"Frances Park's haunted essays are part elegia[...] brothers whispers. She travels from Seoul to Soul via [...] country, the Bayou in Georgetown, a lost cabin in West Virginia, a cosmic dog, creepy neighbors, crazed roommates, old friends, lovers, and her ex (Hug Bug). But it's her mother and lost-too-soon father that steal that show. Grab a vodka-laced Tab and dial up family life in the burbs via pop relics, TV ads, show tunes, dance moves, and chocolate."

    —Richard Peabody, editor of *Gargoyle Magazine*,
       author of *Guinness on the Quay*

"The ferocious energy of Frances Park's essays in *That Lonely Spell*, her lyrical prose, and her poignant subject matter—early loss of her father; isolation as the only Korean family in her Virginia suburb; a complex yet close bond with her mother; and a series of unfulfilling intimate relationships—captivated me from beginning to end. Park's voice is urgent and entertaining. You won't want to miss this collection."

    —R.L. Maizes, author of *Other People's Pets*
       and *We Love Anderson Cooper*

"Frances Park writes so elegantly about family and personal history, and how that history gradually becomes beautiful, monumental myth."

    —Ben Nussbaum, editor of *Spirituality & Health*

"Through the twists and turns of memory, Ms. Park portrays a life lived without restrictions. The tang of childhood makes one wonder what one has missed—were we ever that wide-eyed and accepting? The exuberance of adolescence and young adulthood is told in a wry yet direct manner. Even her mistakes take on the sheen of the bittersweet—how we come to possess our own 'lost paradises.'

A Korean heritage interwoven with an American-upbringing results in unique views on life and family. One cannot imagine a tighter or more loving family environment. The female perspective runs through these stories like an underground river, always present and often rising to the surface. It is a pleasure to read work that combines ethnicity and gender in ways that supersede the default versions of mainstream biographies. These

coming-of-age stories—these life lessons—entertain even as they teach us something about ourselves. Highly recommended."
    —Robert Kostuck, author and editor-in-chief, *DoveTales*

"I can't adequately put into words my praise for *That Lonely Spell*. Each story is magical, so powerful and beautifully recalled you'll swear you were with her."
    —Rick Cooper, lyricist, author of *For the Record*

"A tour de force in memoir writing. Some hard truths spliced with pragmatic humor offer up a book that is informative, elegant, and extravagantly pleasurable to read. Frances Park has lived in many rooms."
    —Susan Tepper, author of *What Drives Men*
        and *The Crooked Heart*, a Play

"*That Lonely Spell* has cast its blissful spell on me like no other essay collection I've read before. Told in a voice that is uniquely hers, each story is heart-tugging and painfully honest—with heaps of humor throughout. Frances Park creates true connection with her readers, leading us, contrary to this book's title, feeling not at all lonely, as if we've just made a new friend. I can't wait to revisit her world and reread her stories from start to finish."
    —Scott Saalman, columnist (*Dubois County Herald*; *Evansville Courier & Press*), author of *What Are You Going to Write About When I'm Gone?*, *Nose Hairs Gone Wild*, and *Mr. Serious*

"While reading *That Lonely Spell*, I found myself wanting to highlight nearly every sentence. Frances Park's stories are deep, blue and soulful—and I loved being lost in her sea of prose."
    —Bill Adler, author of *Outwitting Squirrels* and *Boys and Their Toys*

"*That Lonely Spell* is a luminous collection of stories that covers the beautiful and the brutal in Frances Park's life with the kind of prose that sticks to your bones and stays with you long after you close the book. Emotionally, it packs a huge punch. Books rarely make me cry, but story after story hit me in the heart hard enough to make me tear up. If I had to choose a favorite, I could not. I loved them all."
    —Megan Wessell, blogger, A Bookish Affair

"Frances Park writes in a style that can only be described as rapturous. Reading *That Lonely Spell* brought lots of tears and some laughs as well. She describes events throughout her life with a sense of realism that sometimes entertains, sometimes shocks, and always moves. Her father's premature passing is almost always present, and her love for both parents is evident at all times. I loved every page."
  —Barbra Bailey Bradley, harpist and composer

"The beauty of life comes off like makeup" —to quote from Frances Park's new book *That Lonely Spell*. I would say the beauty of an essay comes off like a short story. These are heartfelt essays that invite you in with warmth and honesty. Reading *That Lonely Spell* is like having a conversation with a friend you wish you had."
  —Carl Scharwath, writer, photographer and competitive runner

"Frances Park's voice as a writer is resonate and authentic."
  —Sandra Tyler, editor-in-chief of The Woven Tale Press,
      author of *Blue Glass* and *After Lydia*

"In this rich and artful memoir-in-essays, Park's loves and losses become the reader's as well. It's a special pleasure to become as happily immersed in the life of another person as I did reading *That Lonely Spell.*"
  —Elizabeth McKenzie, author of *The Portable Veblen*

THAT LONELY SPELL

Stories of Family, Friends & Love

FRANCES PARK

 Heliotrope Books
New York

Copyright © 2022 Frances Park

All rights reserved. No part of this book may be reproduced or transmitted in any form or by any means, electronic or mechanical, including photocopying, recording or by an information storage or retrieval system now known or hereafter invented—except by a reviewer who may quote brief passages in a review to be printed in a magazine or newspaper—without permission in writing from the publisher.

Heliotrope Books, LLC
heliotropebooks@gmail.com

ISBN 978-1-942762-84-3
ISBN 978-1-942762-85-0 eBook

Cover photograph by Justin Redman
Designed and typeset by Naomi Rosenblatt with Frances Park
Interior photographs courtesy of Frances Park

Article Credits

"You Two Are So Beautiful Together" originally appeared in *The Massachusetts Review*/Summer 2016

A Dead Lover's Kiss originally appeared as "Kissed in My Sleep" in OZY/Feb 2016

Meet Me at The Bayou originally appeared in *Gargoyle Magazine*/Issue 65, 2017

A Love Letter to My Sister's Dog originally appeared in *The Delmarva Review*/Fall 2018

Mister, Your Shoelace is Untied originally appeared in Duende/November 2018

Nothing Bad Could Happen Here originally appeared as "Revisiting Childhood Memories, Both Happy and Painful" in Next Avenue/June 2017

I See You, I See You originally appeared in Entropy/October 2016

A Ghost in Edinburgh originally appeared in Mason Street Review/Fall 2020

Good-bye, Tess originally appeared as "Remembering a Free-Spirited Friend" in Next Avenue/January 2018

Serving God, Meat and Intercourse in an Amish Diner originally appeared in *Gulf Coast Journal*/Summer-Fall 2017

A Historic Pause originally appeared in Entropy/June 2017

Kiss-Kiss-Kissuni originally appeared in The London Magazine/September 2016

Death in Andover originally appeared in *The Chicago Quarterly Review*/Fall 2018

Coffee with Catie originally appeared in Entropy/May 2016

Love in Yiddish originally appeared in *Arts & Letters*/Spring 2017

How We Rock 'n' Roll originally appeared in The Woven Tale Press/May 2017

Boobs and Bones originally appeared in Please See Me/March 2020

Between Us originally appeared in Eat, Darling, Eat/February 2021

Koomo Who? originally appeared in *Gargoyle Magazine*/Issue 72, 2020

To the Man I Wish I Married originally appeared as "The One That Got Away" in *O: The Oprah Magazine*/April 2019

That Lonely Spell originally appeared in Spirituality & Health (online)/April 2019, reissued as "Living Through a Lonely Spell" in Next Avenue/August 2019

Finding West Virginia originally appeared in *Spirituality & Health*/July-August 2021

Hey Judy originally appeared as "Remembering a Troubled Childhood Friend" in Next Avenue/September 2017

Slow Dancing with Stan originally appeared in *Folio Literary Journal*/Spring 2020

A Comic Spirit originally appeared in Postcard Poems and Prose/March 2017

"My Heart Will Always Be with You" originally appeared in The Columbia Journal/January 2021

Please note that some of the names of people who have been referenced in these articles have been changed to protect their identity.

To my mom and dad who are waiting for me.
Somewhere.

Contents

Preface/Acknowledgment

"I've always enjoyed listening to people's stories, their history, not the boring bio but the bone-deep stuff, what made them, what broke them."

My little book began seven years ago with a thought: For most of my life, I've been missing my late father badly; one day I thought I'd try my hand at penning a personal essay about him. The piece turned out sweet yet lawless, longer than intended, and titled *Mister, Your Shoelace is Untied*. Another work followed, then another. At heart, they were love letters to my dad and his life, both glorious and cheated.

Others, living and dead, crept into these pages: a stoic maid in postwar Seoul who finally warmed up to me the summer I was seven; a woman who lured me into her basement apartment with the promise of colorful gumballs; a golden boy I never got over; Jefferson, the soulful doodle of my heart; friends cherished, now perished; and of course my mom, alive during most of the writing here, yes, alive and cheering me on with the completion of each story, hot off the press. In the end, I would read twenty-three of the twenty-six essays to her before she left the earth. Our earth. In my mind, my mom will forever be on her sofa in her sitting room, listening hard, really hard while I'm reading with great, measured performance, as English was her third language.

In April 2019, I read her my eponymous essay *That Lonely Spell* in which I describe a sudden emptiness, attributing it to missing an old friend while going through divorce—yet even then I wasn't convinced my reasoning rang true. *You such good writer!* my mom declared, neither of us knowing that day was, in a sense, our curtain call. Within the week she fell unexpectedly ill and by August she was gone. The following March, the pandemic broke out; my beloved shop lights went off, and suddenly the past seven years of writing this book felt cruelly prophetic, leading up to the true lonely spell.

With deep gratitude, I would like to thank my publisher Naomi Rosenblatt who loved this book and believed the whole world would love it, too. Also, to the editors who published my individual stories in their magazines; and to my family and many friends who championed me during dark times and light, most notably my sister Ginger —thank you.

"You Two Are So Beautiful Together"

"So," he grins, "you're saying the two of you smuggled money out of South Korea?"

Hug Bug and I met a little late in life, and, frankly, my husband can't imagine half the things I've done.

"Yes."

"You and your mom."

"That's right."

Ever the historian: "Tell me the story. I've got to hear this."

Okay. In the spring of 1980, my mom and I did just that: smuggled money out of Seoul's Gimpo Airport, holding our breaths until we landed at Dulles airport and deposited the cash in a Washington, DC, bank on Pennsylvania Avenue. Picturing us as partners-in-crime is a laughable picture, a far cry from the shadow we cast, now and then. But with the help of Mr. Chang, a man who'd take a bullet for my father, we did what we had to do.

The Korean police were a brutal bunch in those days, ready to arrest me in a heartbeat—at least, that's how I saw it. A person like me, of Asian face and western manners, was unheard of and not to be trusted. Patrolling police were in airports, restaurants, hotel lobbies—everywhere.

Four years earlier, when my dad was still alive and the family was here for a visit—every three summers—they accosted him at a lake resort, a world away from the soul-crushing sights of Seoul we were escaping that weekend: toddler beggars, lepers, disease, death. You'd think the war ended yesterday, not in 1953. Anyway, the police informed my father that his long-haired daughter walking around in pink shorts was a pornographic shock to their guests, the same guests who swam nude family-style in the lake.

Like they didn't shock *me*?

"Fran," my dad conceded, "from now on, you wear long pants."

"And hair in bun—I can do for you," my mom offered.

Me, hands on hips: "Or else?"

Them, in no uncertain terms: "Or else they kick us out, and we go back to Seoul!"

My parents fell into Korean chatter, and I could usually decipher Korean chatter: My dad was taken aback by the police confrontation. It seems years of living in America had liberalized him. After all, wearing Hawaiian shirts on the weekend was the only way to go.

This visit, too, I felt targeted. By now, my dad had died, and the silhouette of his wife and daughter was drawn: It was just the two of us. In a restaurant in the Chosun Hotel where we were staying, I bummed a Virginia Slims off my mom without a thought.

At this point, I can read Hug Bug's mind: "*You* smoked?"

I was never a true smoker like my mom, who went cold turkey in 1991, the same year she became an American citizen, but there were a few years when I'd occasionally light up to look cool or irreverent. And such a little thing might have gone unnoticed in a male-only room of international types lounging with elite Korean businessmen who'd risen to power in the aftermath of Syngman Rhee's *coup d'etat*; but I'd unwittingly called attention to myself by ordering an OB beer, which was something women just didn't do, not in public and not in private. However, I wasn't thinking, and frankly, I just couldn't resist a Korean beer. Oddly, the color and depth of flavor varied from bottle to bottle, which I found charming in a way that's hard for me to explain, but something along the lines of knowing it came from a little embattled country that could. No matter what hue, it was always delicious.

So, there I was, drinking my OB and lighting a cig when two armed officers approached our table.

"Are you American?"

Did they *ever* play nice?

My mom sat, unusually poised. Whenever we came back to her homeland—although she might argue that point as she was born in the most northern reaches of North, not South Korea—she fell back into character, went from foreign wife to confident, rich girl ice-skating on the Yalu River. Steady, balanced, strong. It was always a stunning transformation.

"Don't worry," she said to me.

She knew Korean law: Only foreigners were allowed to use American products like Virginia Slims. And guess what? I was a foreigner here.

I replied in English, puffing coolly. "Yes, I am. Do you want to see my passport?"

With a sneer, they went back to patrolling.

This always baffled me: If they could tell from across the restaurant that my cigarette was American, you'd think they, like most Koreans, could tell I was American, too. How? By my fashion, look in my eye, and above all, by my sheer size, even sitting down. Maybe friends back home called me "Skinny Minnie," but in a nation of starvation—adults were smaller back then, much smaller—I was the Incredible Female Hulk, a full head taller than Korean females of my generation.

My mom's niece, technically my cousin, though I never thought of her as a cousin, as she was considerably older than me and uncommunicative due to a sad lot in life, was a skilled seamstress in Seoul. Clouded by shame. To make matters worse, she'd recently married some yuck she met on a bus—a lazy, mean drunk who would ruin any promise she ever had. Anyway, wanting to give her some business, we purchased material from a silk house and went to her shop to measure me for jackets—one ruby red, one eggshell. As she unraveled the tape measure around my figure farther than she'd ever unraveled it, her reaction to my big beefy bones—all 112 pounds of me—echoed all over Seoul, bouncing off noodle houses and bathhouses and rotting fruit and fly-infested alleys.

"*Aigoo!*"

If the setting I'm describing sounds more like North Korea than South Korea, keep in mind this was not the Seoul of today but still transitional post-war Seoul. Notions of K-Pop, nightclubs, and Parisian-style bakeries were years from being dreamed up, lit up. Military presence was strong, poverty still ruled—and when I say poverty, hollow-faced children, some naked, some in rags, some curious, most wanting money, all hungry, circling us wherever we walked.

Three things, however, caught my eye, sights I could've never imagined during previous trips: a row of high-rise apartments, a woman in a business suit, and a young couple holding hands.

Slowly, Seoul was changing.

Have I mentioned it was May? It was seven months after my father suffered his fatal stroke in Hawaii, and I'd just turned twenty-five. I thought by this time I was fine, but I know now that "fine" was a fog I'd never quite come out of.

I understood we had business to settle; I wasn't sure what business, and I didn't ask about the amount of money or transactions involved and exact laws we were breaking. The less I knew, the safer I felt, removed from any visions of Korean prisons. You might wonder why we were in such a hurry, why we didn't hold out hope that the laws would change. But here's the thing: How many years did my parents wait for a Reunification Day that would never come?

In my mind, I was just being a good daughter. Whatever my personal shortcomings, when it came to my family, I'd go to the ends of the earth. Period. So, I was here for the ride, escorting my mother into and out of a financially struggling country that wouldn't let her take out what was rightfully hers.

Sort of escorting. As the widow of a World Bank employee, she flew first class while I was relegated to coach.

En route to Los Angeles, when the cabin lights dimmed, and all passengers' eyes were on the in-flight movie, *Running* with Michael Douglas, my mom, in a move I could only call theatrical, threw open the curtain that separated the haves from the have-nots and wandered down the aisle like a tipsy gypsy spirit with her glass of champagne, calling out in the dark:

"Frances! Frances! Where are you?"

"Shhh, Mom!"

"Stewardess say you can come up here to first class!"

The entire coach cabin broke out in laughter. Who we were to each other was obvious.

Even thirty-five years ago, we cut the silhouette of widow mom and daughter. No one had to ask where the husband/father was; you knew that figure was formative but gone and not by desertion but by death, that we were alone everywhere we went and carried his loss on our back. It's been this way for so long I can't recall it being any other way; too long in one sense, not nearly long enough in another. I'm not her only child, and we all have our roles, but I'm the one who took her arm when she lost her husband.

A year or so ago, we were in Safeway near the refrigerated meat section when suddenly, my mom seemed troubled or flustered, maybe by the cuts of flank steak set out or by the price of sirloin, perhaps mismarked. As a vegetarian, it's hard for me to weigh in and talk meat, but honestly, I also just couldn't make out what she was saying. Her English and hearing aren't exactly improving with age, and that only makes her more excitable.

"What is it, Mom?"

"They don't have…I want…"

"What do you want?"

"Newspaper say sale price…"

"Mom, calm down. What exactly are you looking for? I can ask the butcher."

"Where is, I can't find…"

An African American woman was watching us, I realized, watching and smiling. I'd put her age between mine and my mom's. She was also weeping as if a memory had been stirred.

"You two are so beautiful together. So beautiful . . ."

Hug Bug is moved. "What a nice thing to say."

Let it be known I will always love that lady for saying that. I'll hold onto her words like a locket or a crutch or both as my mom and I carry on and carve out our lives year after year without my dad to depend on. On any given day, we make the rounds first to the Asian-Latino market, then to a lunch you eat with chopsticks, and finally to the Korean bakery for chestnut-filled cookies, her favorite, and other *yummy yummies*, as she likes to say.

Yet more than before, my mom's content to spend her days at home where she lives with my younger sister Ginger and her family. Eighty-five in March, she fell down the stairs four years ago and broke her hip—her femur, actually, the body's largest bone. That ticked her off royally.

After surgery, the better part of the day passed before she was wheeled out of intensive care and up to a room. At first, she was her old self with her kids and grandkids, joking, laughing, grateful for no complications, but once everyone went home that night and it was just the two of us, she seemed to fall into an angry hallucinatory monologue. She ranted on about this person and that person; people imagined or half-imagined. The nurses assured me this was normal, just the meds, but around midnight she was really acting up, and I began to panic.

"Mom, listen to me."

"Listen to what?!"

"Do you know who I am?"

"Frances." Pronounced *Fuh-ran-ces*.

"Do you know what happened today?"

Her gaze was a continent away, and it was as if she was trying with all her might to outswim the drugs in her blood and the trauma to her body and swim back to me. Finally, she reached the shore.

"I had a really bad day today, didn't I?"

According to her orthopedist, her recovery was one for the record books. Three weeks post-surgery, she literally tossed her walker during home physical therapy. I wasn't there, but the way Ginger reenacted the scene, our mom was like a shopper getting rid of a bum grocery cart. Good riddance!

"Mrs. Park," the doctor said, "did you see all those people in the waiting room in their wheelchairs? Some are half your age and will never walk again. They could, but they just don't have your will."

My mom, a former high school and college athlete who escaped Communist North Korea at sixteen and crossed a river with bullets stitching the water, scoffed.

"You think I'm gonna be invalid?"

Still, she had to be nursed for a long, long time, and once she got back on her feet, really back on her feet, she was slower. Rain makes her ache; the thought of falling again is paralyzing. Who could blame her? Nowadays, her TV's on more often than not, tuned in to the Tennis Channel or some old wild west channel. Watching *Gunsmoke* and *Wagon Train* episodes from the fifties are a nod to her early days in America as a young wife with somewhere-over-the-rainbow dreams for herself and her husband. The world was beautiful, and good things were coming. And it was, and they did but not for long, and that rainbow's behind her now. Walk by her room—a two-room suite cluttered with all her favorite things—and you'll hear either tennis balls whacking or cowboys and Indians shooting it up. Oh, but she was an outlaw herself, once. And I, her accomplice.

Make no mistake; it was our money to smuggle.

Hug Bug's been wondering: "Where exactly did this money come from?"

At the time, I didn't ask any questions. I didn't think to. But I did understand that taking money out of countries was government-controlled, and the Korean government forbade it. Curious, I called my mom the other day to ask the question. Probe a little. Her response?

"#&!★#"

Story: Behind their backs, her in-laws not illegally but unethically sold a home that wasn't theirs to sell, a near-mansion built in the heart of Seoul and owned by my parents; if anything, more by my mom but women weren't allowed to own property. A wedding gift from her father, he'd purchased it before the war when properties went for a song; the gamble was whether it would still be standing when the bombing ended. As luck would have it, the home remained picture perfect. Not exactly operating like Long & Foster, Korean agencies merely required a signature stamp to seal a deal. Tragically, the in-laws had such a stamp in their possession. So, this home, once rented out to the United Nations and worth a literal gold mine, was sold for a pittance behind my parents' backs for quick cash. We were there to claim what was left over.

During most of our two-week-long stay, I managed to forget about how this trip would all play out in the end: with us smuggling money through customs. For now, we spent time with relatives on her side of the family, took a car into the countryside to visit her father's grave, took a bus even farther out and bought four small hand-carved chests, one for each of her children, and gobbled down appetizers from fragrant food stalls in an underground shopping arcade where grills sizzled with the likes of kimchi pancakes and dumplings I'd kill for today. Kill for.

Hug Bug remarks, "Those sound good."

Exclamation point! One time I made an emergency run at some odd hour because my mom and I had a craving. Got back to the hotel room where we ate like we hadn't eaten for days, mopping up every crunchy, pan-seared morsel with hot sauce.

We also went sightseeing with Mrs. Kim, a hometown friend of my mom's who evidently married well, seeing as she was chauffeured wherever she went. Kind and cultured, she was obviously concerned about her newly widowed friend, not knowing she herself would be widowed in a few short years. Apparently, Mrs. Kim was well aware of our money mission; involved, even though apart from Mr. Chang.

Speaking of whom, our gatherings with Mr. Chang included lunch in a fancy Japanese restaurant and room service tea in our hotel. Not only was he my father's lifelong best friend, but he was also once his college bodyguard (different times, tumultuous political scene), loyal to the end. Presently the CEO of some major Seoul corporation, my mom insisted I'd met him before on previous visits, but frankly, I couldn't distinguish him from my father's other VIP Korean friends— all chauffeur-driven, all dressed in black suits and white suits, all stiff and formal. Not my dad's style. No wonder he separated from the pack and moved to America.

One day, Mr. Chang's limo came to pick us up at the hotel. We were driven to a bank where we were met by him as well as the president of the bank and nine or ten other businessmen. These were my dad's former Yonsei University classmates, gathered here to pay their respects to my mother. As we were shown to a conference room, hundreds of worker-bee heads in their cubicles popped up as we passed by.

Women? Walking with VIPs?

"Why are we here, Mom?"

"Obligation."

We sat at a large conference table. I, the American daughter, vanished like vapor—no one said this wasn't a patriarchal society. At least my mom, wife of Sei-Young Park, held court as Empress.

Here in a bank, I figured financial talk and transactions would come up at the table, but they didn't; indeed, no one in the country was privy to our situation except Mr. Chang and Mrs. Kim. Instead, the talk that day gave way to a sentimental time when these friends were in college, and my dad was the leader of students for political reform, and my mom was the "it" girl they all revered. Gushed with great deference, mind you. My mom, no romantic, couldn't care less, not in college, not at this table. My hunch? She'd rather be knocked and jostled by strangers while dipping *yummy yummies* in hot sauce in the underground shopping arcade.

The last topic of conversation was when they suggested we open the first American franchise in Seoul.

"McDonald's!"

"Baskin Robbins!"

"There is a fortune to be made here!"

An American franchise? In *Seoul*?

My mom and I exchanged a look.

How crazy was that?!

"Oh my God," Hug Bug interjects here, "you two could've been millionaires. Billionaires!"

A few days before our departure, something unsettling happened: Martial Law was declared. Recent student uprisings had tragically resulted in two hundred deaths, and now, at some designated evening hour, everybody had to get off the streets unless you wanted a weapon in your face. I remember looking down from the window of our hotel room and the surreal vision of nothing but uniformed figures—police or soldiers, I can't recall which—patrolling the streets reminded me that I was on the other side of the world. I was ready to go home. So ready.

"When are we going to get the money, Mom? And how are we going to get it?"

"I have already."

"You do?"

"Yah."

The transaction went right over my head, and she seemed to want it that way. The less I knew, the better.

My mom had a Korean passport with a Green Card visa while I had my American passport, and the plan, it turned out, could not have been simpler: to hide the money in our handbags. If we got caught? Play dumb and pray.

Gimpo Airport officials weren't exactly the welcoming committee when you arrived in Seoul. They seemed to get a kick out of harassing "fake" Koreans like us, cursing while examining our luggage and handbags like we were black marketers here to make a killing off that extra can of Maxwell House coffee. I remember them yelling at my siblings and me when we were mere children and once tossing a suitcase so hard the latch broke—no apology.

When you left the country, they checked your luggage but not with a fine-toothed comb. And while they weren't required to check your handbags, they often spot-checked.

The night before we left, I began to fret—I mean, if they spot-checked anyone, wouldn't it be me? The smoker, the drinker, the girl with long hair? Against my better judgment, I looked out the hotel window, down to the streets below. A spooked hush and rows of soldiers did nothing to calm me.

Departure day. Mr. Chang's car showed up at The Chosun Hotel. To my relief, Mr. Chang was inside the limo. We climbed in with our handbags stashed with thousands of American dollars—illegal, of course, to take out of South Korea but within legal limits of bringing into the United States. The two engaged in a conversation that went over my head. The drive from Seoul city to Gimpo Airport seemed longer than it probably was, definitely an eternity to wonder whether we were just being dropped off at the airport or if Mr. Chang was accompanying us inside. When he asked the chauffeur something, I grabbed my mom's arm for dear life.

"Is he coming inside with us?"

"Yah."

"Will he take the fall?"

"What that mean?"

"If we get caught—"

"He say he tell us wrong."

A well-respected man about Seoul not knowing the rules was highly unlikely. But Mr. Chang was devoted to my dad, and, damn it, this was the end.

My mind goes a little blank here. Spotty. And like this story, not to mention my memory, if there are a couple of holes here and there like how and when the money exchange from Korean *won* to American dollars was handled, it's because there are. But probe my mom again? She'd rather watch *The Big Valley* in peace than push the mute button and dig up ancient history.

What I do recall is that the Gimpo Airport officials looked particularly steely that day, and my nerves rippled through me and into my mom, for she began to shiver then shake—we were that close. My cool assurance back in the restaurant was one thing; after all, it was within my rights to smoke a Virginia Slims, but smuggling money out of the country was another matter. Even if they didn't arrest us, they could confiscate the cash—and then what?

I also recall Mr. Chang standing behind a roped area along with other people waving good-bye to their friends and family. Like a hawk watching his brood fly to safety, his eyes were on me and my partner-in-crime, and on some plane—no, no, not the kind with wings—we were all together, holding our collective breaths and only as I'm finishing up this story does it dawn on me what Mr. Chang might have done had we been caught: bribe the officials. Yes, that had to be it.

As it turned out, we sailed through customs—a miracle!—without anyone checking our handbags. Maybe the Gimpo Airport officials were thinking: *Get out! Go back to America!*

Hug Bug interrupts me. "Wait a minute. It all sounds too easy. Too smooth."

"What are you saying?"

"It seems like they turned a blind eye."

"What do you mean?"

"I mean, I bet Mr. Chang had *already* bribed the Korean officials. Think about it."

I'm thinking about it, and he may be right. But there's no way to know, not now.

Out of the danger zone, my mom and I headed toward the gate when she abruptly stopped, turned around, and waved good-bye to Mr. Chang. Her face grew sad.

"I never see him again," she said.

"Why not?"

"I never come back here."

And she never has.

Every year, for years, my mom would receive a Christmas card in the mail from Mr. Chang, always with a personal message about how much he missed my father. In one, he wailed, *Every day I wake up and say to myself, is he really gone?*

One year, no Christmas card arrived, and we knew Mr. Chang was gone, too.

I feel bad for saying I couldn't distinguish him from the other Korean VIPs. He was my dad's best friend.

Eventually, in a circuitous hush-hush scheme, my mom got all her cash out of the country. Apparently, she'd left a Korean bank check with Mrs. Kim in good faith, which got the money ball rolling. Beyond that, I'm a bit cloudy, and while I've already asked my mom a few times now about how exactly the money was channeled, all I can really decipher is that it involved Mrs. Kim's husband and a Los Angeles associate of his who ended up sending her a check for the full amount.

"Was there a letter with it?" I asked her.

"No. Just note on check."

"What did it say?"

"*Here is money we owe you.*"

"Hm," my husband says.

A cryptic note, indeed.

If there are more cryptic notes to this story, in the end, it doesn't matter. Thirty-five years later, that cloak-and-dagger moment in an airport is so far behind us even our shadows cast shadows. And guess what? We're still here, a silhouette of widow mom and daughter etched in stone.

Still beautiful together.

"What a great story," Hug Bug says. "Will you read it to me again?"

A Dead Lover's Kiss

I like to think W wasn't a bad person, just a troubled one. Oh, we had good times, sweet times, fell to our knees silly in that furniture store that sold factory seconds where three-legged tables went for a song, but sometimes his eyes went cruel blue and wouldn't let you in—not even at knifepoint, I bet. Stone cold upon hearing of his father's death, he cried whenever "Desperado" came on the radio like it meant something to him and only him, too precious to share with me, and hey, I was only the girl he called Face, the girl he wanted to marry. So, W was cut deep but so what when it was the ruin of him.

"Why do you always cry when you hear that song?"

"Leave me alone, Face."

We met because he was the most beautiful thing I'd seen in a long time. My lips, painted siren red, what else, in those days, couldn't wait for that moment alone when I'd suffocate him with so many kisses he'd look like Bozo, and so I gave him a look on a crowded DC street. You never think a look in 1988 will lead to something historic enough to write about, though now I wished he never noticed.

"Can I take you to dinner?"

"Take me anywhere."

Early on, we went for a drink at Duke Zeibert's. Next to us was a woman with a brassy laugh, aching for love. When W got up to use the men's room, Brassy leaned over to me:

"My God, you're the luckiest woman alive."

W was a pretty boy, though subtly rough around the edges from smoking, drinking, late nights. His throat was gravel, his jeans frayed. Unlike me, who longed to write like Janis Joplin sang, more fascinated with the dream world than the waking, W lived for happy hour, which I blamed on his dad, helpless and bedridden but in his heyday a mean drunk who would take W, his little towhead, to other women's apartments while he did his thing. Well, like father like son, and I should've run, but a girl can't always be of sound mind, even when the boy inherited a faithless carriage—you can always tell by the way someone moves. So, despite my suspicions, I stayed. Indeed, a year later, we moved into a house on a lake with glittery views.

　　"C'mon, let's get married, Face!"

　　"I don't think so . . ."

When his dad was on his deathbed, we were summoned to his childhood home, where a priest was delivering last rites. Afterward, W refused to join the sobbing circle in the living room where his mom and sisters were confiding dark family secrets to the priest. Instead, W busied himself in the garage while I eavesdropped from the kitchen. Later, I confronted him:

　　"Your sisters said your father used to beat you to a bloody pulp every day—is that true?"

　　"Hell, no. Never."

In time, I walked out on W. His ludicrous denials of cheating and other drama did me in, left me looking worn and alcoholic, and asking myself how I ever could've loved such a person. In self-imposed exile, I didn't date or drink for years and barely spoke to a soul, just wrote my heart out. I went vegetarian, vowing to renew myself on a cellular level but instead fell sick with a mysterious virus that attacked every inch of me, body and soul. I thought I would die before I would ever recover.

　　Meanwhile, W begged me to come back, and I didn't get it and still don't get it. Now he was free to fuck whomever, free to get trashed and weep without question to "Desperado," so do it, man, and fall off a cliff while you're at it, I don't care.

　　One day, two years later, I heard a knock at the door. W: his car was at the curb. More knocks, but I didn't answer, and finally, they stopped. He wouldn't leave, though, just sat in his car looking paralyzed. Should I scream? Call the police?

　　Suddenly, he jumped out, slammed his car door shut, and began knocking again so furiously it knocked the fear right out of me. Ready to strangle him, I cracked the door open and saw his wasted soul.

　　"Go away."

　　"Can't I just check on you once in a while, Face? See how your writing's going?"

"Go away. Forever."

And he did. Sort of.

In 2010, I was in the middle of a work when my editor at St. Martin's suggested I was holding back. More personal details, please; readers want that, crave that, hear about your love life. Problem was, I'd always been embarrassed by my W chapter, if you will; it always seemed like a character slip on my end. A DUI, a black mark. What would my readers think of me?

Only that I was human.

Still, chronicling my time with W was so weird after twenty years; molecularly removed, I could only remember two strangers from some foreign moon. Out of curiosity, I googled W and what popped up was shocking: his death notice in the *Washington Post*, published that very day. Every atom in me crumpled like paper.

Soon after that, I dreamt I was in my kitchen when W appeared, standing closer to me than humans can. His face dove down to mine as he whispered "I'm sorry" in a voice so broken, so haunting, only a devil would push him away; then kissed my cheek. I woke up with two sensations: a hot tear running down my face and a little fire where his lips were. And there I lay like ashes.

Meet Me at the Bayou

There are still times while slipping into REM—the dream stage, not the band—when I find myself back on that treacherous staircase from hell as if it's still there, and I'm still in strappy high heels negotiating each step down. I'm in a fog, a voodoo fog. *Don't fall, don't fall, don't you dare friggin' fall...* Yet I do, always, lose my footing then jerk awake under the sheets.

Crazy, I know.

The actual set of steps, steep and narrow and a mile long in memory, led from the main floor to the balcony level of the Washington, DC, nightclub where I worked one summer as a cocktail waitress. Part of the job was looking cool, not tripping flat on your face, though frankly, you couldn't slip through the cracks if you tried, given the trains of people jamming both directions. Party! Still, it instilled something in me with staying power; wobbly and fearful and beyond my realm. Yet it makes no sense, as I was having the time of my life, ever conscious of my finger on the pulse of what it meant to be alive that iconic moment in time, movin' and groovin' along with everyone else. Riding the American rock 'n' roll wave in those days possibly meant more to me than you, but don't worry, this isn't that story. Not really.

This is the story, no, backspace, not a story, a glimpse, a dreamy sliver from the summer of 1976. And if I've lost the writing fire of my youth, so be it—no flowery prose or highbrow poetics goin' on here. Don't need no imagination cuz this ain't fiction. It all happened at The Bayou.

Located under the Whitehurst Freeway in an old building on the Georgetown waterfront—a neglected plot in those days—the legendary club was known for premier house bands that electrified the stage, two levels of dance floors and bars, $1.10 cocktails, and unapologetic debauchery. Loud and cavernous, before its incarnation as The Bayou, it apparently had a storied and checkered past, unclear to me, but something about a mob hit back in the thirties, I think. During daylight hours when the joint was deserted, ghosts, very shady ghosts, likely roamed their old haunt. But the seventies were my era, and I can tell you there still wasn't a polished note in the hazy, votive candle-lit air—everybody drank and smoked and did unspeakable things in the dark, you didn't think not to. Our families in 'burbs such as my home-town of Springfield eating Colonel Sanders Kentucky Fried Chicken and watching *Happy Days* would choke on their chicken bones.

Just x-ed out a line about remembering every corner like yester-day because I'm no historian, and whatever I'm reliving is obviously dimmed by time and mental mist. Consider this: My recollection that the steps were wooden and creaky as skeletons is seared in my soul, but if you said, "No, darlin', they were concrete or marble or covered by a burgundy booze-soaked carpet," I wouldn't argue. On the other hand, though The Bayou was infamously razed in 1999, I'll leave my memories standing. Don't we always?

Monday night was Blues Night when the Nighthawks took the stage and played honky-tonk, hell-raisin', foot-stompin' sets shades of Little Feat that could make an old biddy boogie. Tuesday night was Ladies' Night when guys on the prowl got girls with Charlie-per-fumed hair drunk on fifty-five-cent drinks. The other nights were so busy they didn't need a name, packing in more bodies on two thump-ing floors than fire code allowed. Bands like Face Dancer, Sinbad, and Cherry People (or was it Cherry Smash or both?) rocked cover songs from Pink Floyd and Led Zeppelin and Yes and David Bowie, etc. All album material, some original compositions, no disco shit. Wanna know something? I can actually hear "Dark Side of the Moon" as I'm typing this. . .

The music, amped up and deafening, brought out the zoo in you, and suddenly this was life, real life, high voltage just the way it was meant to be—yeah!—and nearly every face I'd ever known in my twenty-one years seemed to pass through these doors during one of my shifts or another as I, soaking up the magic as I was living it, snaked my way through the madding crowd on the balcony level where I claimed a station for two reasons.

One, the ladies' room was here—an easy scoot, no stairs to face. Decrepit glam, it was a throwback to the thirties with an enormous powder room that housed a dozen or so parlor chairs facing an L-shaped mirror (or was it U-shaped?) crowded with female reflections all hair, lipstick, and chatter. Two, I liked it up here where the tone was a pitch more civilized. You could even catch your breath every so often as you held a tray high above your head, balancing Michelobs and Tom Collins and Screwdrivers while racing back and forth from table to bar all night till two a.m. Before the end of the first week, I went down two jean sizes.

Night One, I walked around in a white tube top with pink-coral bells, hair swept up in a long ponytail revealing dangly earrings plus a ruby stud for statement. The look was tied together with a sweet little white apron my mom made for me—my tip drawer, you might say. She was a whiz with a sewing needle, having spent part of her schoolgirl days making uniforms for the Imperial Army when Korea was under Japanese Occupation and then later in life shortening the arms of her husband's shirts—in their early days here, you couldn't find clothes off the rack in Korean-man size. Anyway, my ensemble wasn't exactly thrown together as my younger sister Ginger vividly recounts me modeling my outfits in front of the mirror for hours on end. I guess I went to great lengths to feel beautiful, even if I feared it was all an ornamental lie. But mirror model today? For my wedding last year, I picked out a dress online—granted, a gorgeous shimmery dress—and tried it on only once before the Big Day.

Ah, but this was then. *Every* day was a big day. Or night. Can't forget the sparkly lip gloss and dressed-up eyes, much to my dad's chagrin. For the longest time, he pictured me at ten forever, a Madame Curie in the making. When he realized I favored pen and paper over Bunsen burners, *Even better, Fran!* A voracious reader hungry for signs of meaningful life—Tolstoy, Saint Augustine, Pearl Buck—he was already having delusions of my grandeur before my eleventh birthday.

My Fran will be world-renowned!

I'm wincing as I type this: Had my father lived to see the sale of my novel announced in the *New York Times*, no one would've been prouder. And had he lived to see that same book in the Dollar Store a few years later, no one's heart would've cracked louder.

Now that I'm his age when he passed away, older even, I wonder what he made of a bookish daughter who began to show signs of a party girl who loved to come alive after midnight. I think it bothered him, it must have, but he wouldn't let it bother him too much. Keeping peace was always preferable even when his face was a megaphone: *My Fran doesn't need makeup!*

But, of course, I did, and here's a story whose humor may be lost in the telling: One time, as a teenager, I was sitting next to him in our white Pontiac Tempest in the driveway. I'm zoning in here and to understand this sentiment you'd have to know first-hand the cruelty of strangers, so cruel I'd be happy to hear they were all dead: Our world in this warm little sacred cube was ours, all ours. No one could hurt me here. I was safe.

About to turn on the ignition, he hesitated.

"Close your eyes, Fran."

A gift? It wasn't my birthday. I couldn't read his mood but, if anything, it seemed playful, and I closed my eyes, expecting a surprise but not exactly the one I got. In a move as uncharacteristic as him breaking into the Bump in The Bayou, he wiped my eyelids clean of Maybelline.

"There's my Fran!"

But tonight, I was boss, in full glitter and glory. Whenever I bounced by one particular table, I'd hear, "Hey, Miss Universe!"

Turn the clock back to 1962 when I would slip on my mom's white high heels and pretend I'd just been crowned Miss America, holding imaginary roses and crying with joy—*Thank you, thank you!* Seeing as I was who I was, the coronation was laughable on every level. Fast forward to 1976.

"Hey, Miss Universe!"

You only own that title once in your life, so smile. Oh, but they could never have me; that was the power, that was the high.

Not that I was an angel but compared to the other cocktail waitresses who were rougher around the edges and well-acquainted with the underbelly of club life, I was. Another difference was that for me, the only college girl, this was a rockin' dream summer job, a wild scene but make no mistake, not my life. I wouldn't be doing this when I was twenty-*two*, for God's sake. Oh, wait, there was another college girl, an art student from New York whose name escapes me but not her exquisite Jacqueline Bisset looks, ruined whenever she opened her mouth.

"So, these guys promised me a ride home tonight if I partied with them after work. D'ya think I can trust them?"

That night and a couple of other nights early on, she asked if I could drive her home to a group house in Georgetown where she was living that summer. She was mindful of giving me gas money—a quarter, your average tip per drink—which was decent of her, and I took it because a quarter was measurable money back then.

If I wasn't the only college girl, I was definitely the only cocktail waitress with a foreign face—nothing new; mine was unique everywhere I went, so I held it high. I was also, as far as I could tell, the only girl who had no interest in sleeping with the band, so to say. In my own head, my insecurities blared louder than any Bose speaker, but I'd rather barrel down the staircase in front of a packed house than show them to anyone, much less to some musician who'd played with my boobs and then dumped me. During a training period that lasted all of ten minutes, I overheard all I needed to hear:

"I went to bed with him, and now the bastard acts like he doesn't know me. What do I do? How can I get him back?"

Momentarily, the cocktail waitress in tears was circled by her comrades, all obviously well-versed in humiliation. Right then, I knew my place wasn't inside their circle, and I honestly can't recall a conversation with any of them except for the art student who didn't last the whole summer. Being outside the circle, any circle, was where I was most comfortable, anyway. When you're different, you don't assume you'll be invited to the party, you don't even assume your second-grade teacher will treat you nicely, which she didn't, so unless someone throws themselves at you, you never say a word. In that sense, you're always a loner, even in the company of friends, to some degree. Jeez, why am I saying *you*? Of course, I mean *me*, who never once came across another Korean American student during my entire education, from kindergarten through college.

But back to the local rock gods with great hair and sexy moves. Even if they were sweet guys with college degrees, I was always more drawn to the thinker in the corner, then and now. My husband, whom I picture as a baby in a crib full of books, not blankets, has lamented to me on more than one occasion:

"Why wasn't I in DC that summer? We could've met at The Bayou and had ten grandchildren by now."

He's joking. Isn't he? At any age, fifty-eight or twenty-one, Hug Bug would've never stood in line, flashed his ID, paid a cover charge—$1.50 on weekdays, $2.00 on the weekends—and entered the divine dive that was The Bayou, not in this life or the one after that or the one after that, period. Mentally, we were on different planets; he, studying in Jerusalem and me, serving up drinks at a nightclub. Circling different moons. Still, he claims that *had* our paths crossed, it would've been love at first sight. He's joking. He must be.

Now that first night, I did meet a boy, handsome but a bit conservative, with preppy brown hair and a shirt vaguely disco. From his first line, Peter was curiously familiar to me, a Boston boy with a girl-crazy Bahhston persona. Our comic bond was instant.

"Vahhka Tahhnic, please!"

"Uh, I don't think so!"

Why the exclamation points, you ask? We were shouting over the music!

"Why nahht!?"

"I don't see a stamp on your hand!"

"I'll be twenty-one ahhn July 17!"

"Hey, that's my dad's birthday!"

"It's in the stahhs!"

"Are you from Boston?"

"Bahhston bahhn and bred!"

"I was born there, too!"

"What'd I tell you? It's in the stahhs!"

But of course, the stars. A little gleam in your eye can make you stay in a moment.

"Wanna dance?"

"Sorry! I can't dance until midnight!"

Midnight was the magic hour when cocktail waitresses, if we didn't mind losing two hours of tips, could rip off our aprons and hit the dance floor. Having spent my preteen years dreaming of being a go-go dancer on Hullabaloo while listening to WPGC or spinning 45s on a blue and white polka dot record player, yeah, you might say I loved to dance.

Years earlier, my dad, a World Banker who traveled too much, re-layed a sweet story to me: He was in London one day when a pop song wafted out of a clothing boutique on Carnaby Street, a song that reminded him of his daughter a-go-go in a rec room across the ocean. He went in, coming out with a very mod-looking top, lime green with sequins, something Twiggy would wear. The wow factor told me a shopgirl had picked it out for my dad.

"I felt like you were with me, Fran."

For years, the top stood out in my closet like neon. When I think about it now, I grow sad.

Of the two dance floors at The Bayou, I preferred the one on the main level. It was bigger with more exposure; even people leaning over the balcony railing were watching, and I liked that, all those eyes on us. At this age, dancing for me was a kind of striptease of the soul: look but don't touch. My moment, however, was often upstaged whenever this one particular girl would show up. A blonde baby doll, she could boogie like it was nobody's business. Damn. I was gonna be outdanced.

Hug Bug, bless his sweet lying heart, says I still have the moves even when the moves are more Frankensteinian than seductive. But I'm digressing...

"Wanna pahhty when you get off?"

"Sorry! I have a boyfriend!"

Off and on, anyway. His name was Jack; we both went to Virginia Tech and were home for the summer, but the love wasn't there no matter how many times we said it. Far from the greatest story ever told, we were good in bed, and he would soulfully sing and strum "I Will"—my favorite Paul song—on demand. So, some good times, but not love, never love. Without digging deep here, our history had made us resentful and immature and say some really shitty things you can never take back so no surprise that midway through my Bayou stint, we broke up—again—and I began spending time with Peter, during and after hours. A little dancin' and romancin', sweet and harmless, was just what the doctor ordered. A student at UMass, he was working as an intern for the Treasury Department, his second summer in a row, doing all the right things against what I sensed was a quelled wild streak. Over and over, as if detecting a tremor from a future quake, he'd deliver with heart-crushing angst:

"Francie, I don't want to end up working for the government and getting married and settling down in the suburbs. I don't want to do it. That's just not who I am."

Me, neither. IN ALL CAPS.

"Then don't, Peter. No one's making you do it."

He would do all those things by age thirty; settle into a conventional life with a smile.

In 2001, Peter wondered if we could meet for lunch, having run into me through the years, not at The Bayou but here and there in the 'burbs and the city, occasionally even wandering into a sweet little fabled chocolate shop I happen to co-own with my sister. His first time in, it was as a customer.

"Do you take Mastercahhd?"

In the quarter-century since we'd actually sat down together, not a minute seemed to have passed. We were twenty-one again, just like that. The space we'd carved out for ourselves so long ago was still there after all these years, waiting for us to flesh out again. Not for dancin' or romancin', just to say, "Hey, our time together was special, wasn't it?" After lunch, my parting words were:

"Meet me at The Bayou."

He smiled, still handsome, going gray.

These days, I'm still in touch with both Peter and Jack in an "I'm-still-in-this-world-and-you're-still-in-this-world" kind of way. Not in a way either would ever offer to save me from a fall, not in real life and not in my dreams. But once upon a time, I could count on one or the other to visit me during my shift and stay with me till closing and funny how in memory, however flawed, it gives me a warm fuzzy feeling to revisit those late nights when one or the other would help me blow out votive candles, place empty beer bottles back into their appropriately labeled cases, prop chairs on tables, upside down. I'd retrieve my tip money from my apron and count it like a poor pau-pette. Then it was time to climb down that staircase, holding onto the railing for dear life.

The summer after I met Peter, a girlfriend and I decided on a spur-of-the-moment to drive up to Boston to spend Thanksgiving with my relatives. From a phone booth in Harvard Square, I called to see if he was home. His dad answered. It was my only conversation with the man, but I remember his voice, the voice of a good man; I understand he passed away quite a while ago. Jack's father died last week and that he outlived my dad by thirty-five years is a crime, enough said. And then there's Esther, the only friend in present day I could imagine with me at The Bayou way back when and maybe even now, let our hair down and dance with strangers and sing, just for one lawless night, *We don't have birthdays anymore, we're like the store—Forever 21.* She lost her dad, an esteemed Princeton professor, to cancer just a few months ago. At least he lived to grow old and see grandchildren.

So, all fathers go, but mine went first.

The night before I went away to college—not cross country, just cross state—I went out with friends. It seemed like the thing to do; party and say good-bye. When I left the house, my dad was on the couch in the living room, the same place he often sat to read and be alone with his thoughts, though there were times he'd ask me to join him so we could talk about life. He was nursing a drink, most likely a scotch, his drink of choice.

"Bye, Dad."

"Bye, Fran."

Hours later, when I returned, he was still there, in the same spot. I didn't know what he'd been doing or what was going through his mind, whether that was the same scotch or another one. But I did know it was hard for him to let his children go.

One night, I forgot my apron. There was probably an extra apron or a jar behind the bar where I could stash my tips. The minor emergency would have been forgotten by morning if not for one thing. Fairly early into my shift, I heard:

"Your dad's downstairs!"

Downstairs…

Downstairs…

Downstairs…

My dad? In *The Bayou*? Why, for God's sake? To my knowledge, my father had never driven to partying Georgetown; how did he know how to even get here? Where did he park? I couldn't picture him, a dignified man—much less a dignified Korean man—in The Bayou. How insulting to his senses. How mortifying to mine. When you walked in here, you pretty much abandoned who you were in the 'burbs. Yanked out of one dimension and into another, no doubt I stood at the top of the staircase, ready to trip my ass off.

Don't fall, don't fall, don't you dare friggin' fall…

When I saw my dad—there he is, near the entrance—it was like spotting a polar bear in Hawaii. *It can't be.* My identity as his daughter went up in smoke with my painted lips, eyes done up to dazzle in the dark. Would he even recognize me?

"Fran!"

He waved my way, seemingly oblivious to the stomping audience and ear-splitting amps, the crazed haze that was The Bayou.

"Fran!"

Suddenly it was just the two of us in our walled-off, incubated world. We may as well have been in the living room discussing Tolstoy.

"Dad," I said, noticing something in his hands, "what are you doing here?"

"I brought your apron."

"You drove all the way from Springfield to bring me my *apron*?"

Whenever my college friends got letters from home, they were always from their moms. But my dad wrote me, too, whenever he had a moment to spare, whether from his desk at the World Bank during his lunch hour or the Erawan Hotel in Bangkok before bed. Sharing his reflections du jour was a calming pastime for him.

"Yah, Fran. You left it on the banister."

My sister Ginger, then a pipsqueak of thirteen, insists she had come along for the ride and was at The Bayou, too, that night, with our dad. But I can't see her. Underaged, maybe she wasn't allowed past the entrance. Maybe time blurred her from the picture.

"Thanks, Dad," I said, backing up into the bowels of The Bayou to return to duty. What else was I supposed to do? Invite him in? "Drive home carefully, OK?"

"Yah."

A thought comes to mind: Had I known I would lose him to a stroke three years later, lose him forever, I would've dropped my apron, run out of The Bayou, and grabbed my father so hard he could've never left this Earth, not even if God, the angels, and fate willed it.

While trying to make sense of a staircase probably more menacing in memory, I'm reminded of something Esther said to me. We're women with little free time, so when we get together, each minute feels sacred and secret. *Talk to me. No one's listening.* Last November, just before Thanksgiving, she stopped by my shop to pick me up, along with some chocolate treats. Then we went for coffee at Au Bon Pain a block away. The hour was dusk.

Divorced now for a couple of years, she began telling me about a man she was seeing. Red flags went up left and right, but I held my tongue as she, in a charming if not absent manner, arranged little nuggets of chocolate-covered toffees on a napkin as if we were sitting down to a game of chess. But the game of love was what she was really playing, and she needed to make a move. Red flags wave forever. And no one's Forever 21.

"Run," I said.

Hoping for some reaction, she, no meek woman, added meekly, "The sex is good."

"Run."

"Doesn't that count for something?"

"No, Esther. Run."

She nodded airily, moving her chocolate nuggets around, eating one or two in the process and still talking about him as if to convince the universe he was worth a little more time. But at our ages, you don't play with candy. You do that when you're young, and it's fun. In the middle of a sentence, her face changed.

"As I say this all aloud, it's so clear to me."

As I put this all on paper, it's so clear to me now, too: Some nights when I'm drifting off, the beauty of life comes off like makeup, and I know in my heart of hearts, my darkest heart, the one beating at the top of a staircase, that I'm no longer safe, and my dad will never, ever meet me at The Bayou again.

A Love Letter to My Sister's Dog

Mama had a dream last night, Jefferson. You were still alive but barely, your liver failing, your shaven belly mustard yellow, and the vets said there was nothing they could do, so we brought you home, and we gave you a bath where something biblical happened: the water washed away your jaundice. As Mama told me about her dream, every cell in me stirred because it was like her love for you. Powerful. Mine, too, though I know I'm just Mama's sister whose visits were cameo appearances that began with a car beep. *Baby's here!* You went nuts whenever you heard that, didn't you? Howled your head off! And whenever I began to gather my things to go, you'd grow quiet. Disgruntled. *Traitor.* You know, Jefferson, a person can't count on many things in life, but as I'd begin to drive away, slowly, my foot barely on the pedal, the chance that you'd be staring back at me through the window was always excellent. I'd brake, and our eyes would lock like magnets and we'd stay in that pull for a long time. In a way, that's as deep as it goes. Famous friends, not like you and Mama, I'm not delusional, you two were twin-spirits roaming this plane and the next if there is a next, Mama and Jefferson forever . . . though sometimes your attachment was extreme and you'd become so glum we'd say *Jefferson's on suicide watch!* because you'd lie in bed all day, not eating, not moving, just waiting for her to come home. Mama aside, when it was just you and me, we occupied a special space, a poetic place with your paw over my wrist. Didn't we? By the way, Jefferson, when I say we gave you a bath—in Mama's dream, I mean—she didn't say whether "we" included me, but I like to think I was there, in dream life, helping to rinse death off you.

Wherever you are, I want you to know I'm writing this on a gray January morning, spheres removed from that dreamy day when your parents and brother picked you up at the airport and brought you home in a puppy crate. You were something called a goldendoodle— your brother had allergies and, well, it boiled down to a poodle, a doodle, or nothing. Our family had been dog-less for a quarter-century, which was fine with me—confession: I was never a true dog lover, always thought they were a bit of a bother—but after work, the summer sky still light and bright, I stopped by just to catch a glimpse of you. A *what* doodle? A decade ago, that was all you were to me. Not that it was love at first sight for you, either.

So, there you were, and will always be, a beautiful little lamb, a red-collared pup on all fours, refusing to face us. Wherever we set you down, on the grass, on the floral rug, you'd make an about-face, taking orders from your instincts. Paralyzed. I guess if I was plucked from a peaceful farm in Oregon and took a loud scary plane ride for five hours, I'd turn away, too, but . . . I also think that's how God made you. Introverted. Stony to strangers. Your love, once bloomed, was reserved for us, your family. That drew me in; made you and your love more special. Some things I found so fetching: The way you'd position yourself so my hair would fall on your face whenever Mama trimmed my ends. The way you growled whenever my husband hugged me— *Hands off* my *Baby!* You were a thinker, like my long-gone dad, and call me nuts, but were you trying to tell me something with those soulful brown eyes? Oh, if paws could write . . . Spiritual, too, in a doggy way. Sometimes you broke into a crazy—OK, I'll just say it— *possessed* bark, and if I didn't know better, I'd swear you were barking at ghosts dancing around my head.

Granted, you could be dogs-just-wanna-have-fun, too.

Give me treats!

Hide my tennis ball!

Take me to Hidden Pond!

Ah, Hidden Pond. Granted, you loved your home, especially your spot by the big lumpy elephant-gray sofa, but mention Hidden Pond and everything flew out the window. It was your favorite place in the world where your soul became one with every enchanting rock, trail, stream, and falling leaf. Hearing Mama say *Let's go to Hidden Pond!* could awaken you from your deepest sleep.

Well, almost.

I'm regretting something right now, Jefferson. I rarely went to Hidden Pond with you, just a couple of times, and always opting for the easy trail otherwise known as the Orange Path, which cheated you a little. The Green Path, your trail of choice, was too long and treacherous for me. Believe it or not, I started out life as a tomboy who could outrun and outjump any boy in class, a skateboarding fiend, but then I got all poetic and lost myself in words not woods and emerged a rock in some ways yet a delicate flower in others—ugh, I agree. Maybe Mama can hop over steep rocks while eating gummy bears, but I'd fall into some crevice and never be heard from again.

By your tenth birthday, you could still pass for a fluffy puppy, but then, abruptly, you slowed down. The staircase was a struggle, each step a crawl-hop. Once, after a long walk in Hidden Pond, your legs gave out and you had to be lifted into the car. Born with hip dysplasia, you had surgery early on, but here it was, back to haunt you. Oh, you were such a good boy at the vet acupuncturist office last summer, model-still with all those needles sticking out of your doodle fur, but worth it because your breed's lifespan is fifteen years. Miraculously, the acupuncture worked.

Back to Hidden Pond!

With a spring in your step!

True, your walks were abbreviated now. That majestic tree, the grandest in Hidden Pond standing like some ancient Tree of Life, now marked the end of your journey. Time to turn around.

But, damn it all, one day in mid-December, you stopped eating. The following afternoon you were admitted to the animal hospital—your bilirubin levels were high, pointing to liver disease. The next night, Saturday night, Mama and I went to visit you, though she'd been in and out all day. The hospital staff and décor tried to be cheery but failed miserably; frankly, I had bad vibes as we waited in a room with a maroon rug for an eternity—you weren't going to get well here. Finally, a nurse walked you in. You plopped down, your shaven belly and ankles and the whites of your eyes dark yellow. Worst, your expression was gone.

Where were you, Jefferson?

Just before we left, you perked up in a pup-like way only because you had to pee bad, really bad, so Mama leashed you, and the two of you charged out of the room, through the hospital lobby and automatic front doors, leaving me in the dust. Suddenly it was like it always was, Mama and Jefferson together forever, and what I'm about to tell you will break Mama's heart when she reads this: Something about the starless vision of your silhouettes running into a pitch-black night shook every molecule in me, and all I was thinking was, *Run you two, keep running, somewhere, anywhere, don't turn around, even if it means you never come back because if you come back, Jefferson will never get out of this deathtrap alive and the dream will be over.*

I was wrong. You came home on Monday, the same day I developed a cough, easy to ignore at a time like this. The hospital vets said there was nothing more they could do except give you meds and *let's see what happens.* Uh, five thousand dollars later, and *let's see what happens?* What happened was an emotional rollercoaster: one hour you were walking around the block, the next hour your legs buckled; one hour you were barking at the television, the next hour one breath from death. *Jefferson,* I'd say, knowing you'd come to life if only for a split second, *you've got to get better so we can go to Hidden Pond!*

What happened, in the end, is that on Friday, December 23, at ten in the morning, eight days after you stopped eating, the in-home euthanasia vet arrived with his assistant. I'm telling you this because I'm not sure how conscious you were, lying on the floral rug, Jefferson. You seemed at peace, even ready to leave us, but when I later learned you were doped up on morphine, I wasn't so sure of anything anymore. Maybe you were in some drugged-induced state, dreaming of Hidden Pond. All I know is that you surrendered to the vet's needle without a stir. In case you weren't aware of those last moments, your grief-stricken Mama was sobbing *Mama loves Jefferson, Mama loves*

Jefferson, petting you so feverishly no doubt you'll feel her love forever. When you were gone, she collapsed on you, and I, her sister shadow, collapsed on her. You know, Jefferson, I never got to say good-bye to my dad; he was here then gone forever. So, despite the tragic hour, I'm grateful I could say good-bye to you.

Her next blink, your inconsolable Mama began lamenting, *Where is Jefferson now? I need a sign he's OK . . .*

I'm not a religious person, not by a longshot, and only in dream life could a baptismal bath wash away your jaundice. But signs of afterlife, I've had a few, and I'm not talking about when someone's thinking about their dead friend Mike, and then a Michael & Son truck happens to drive by—God, no, that's not what I mean. I mean something tangible and magical when you least expect it. Yet poor Mama couldn't wait—*Baby, I need a sign he's waiting for me now.* I could believe she might get her sign from you someday, but not today, not this soon.

On Christmas—two days after you left this earth—your parents and brother went to Hidden Pond in your honor. I would've gone too—you know that, Jefferson—but by now, my cough had progressed to bronchitis. Their original plan was to walk the Green Path trail to the majestic tree, scatter some of your ashes along the way, but Mama couldn't bring herself to give any of you away, and I don't blame her.

When your family reached their landmark, they discovered something that wasn't there last time, something uncanny: On a bed of leaves in the crook of the tree's hollow, nestled if not deeply rooted, sat a tiny pup with a red collar; a figurine, of course, too sacred to touch, of ancient thistle or twine, Mama guessed. The figurine, Jefferson, was you. At least the image of you just out of your crate one long-ago summer day.

Now, if that wasn't Mama's sign from beyond the universe, then signs just don't exist.

Well, Jefferson, under cursed skies, my little ode to you comes to a close. It's still January, and I'm still coughing here—that's how fresh your loss feels. However silly, a part of me wants to hold onto the cough as if otherwise your memory and a bewitching figurine will fade into a dream or a myth. No, not a chance. Maybe I'm not Mama, but I cried writing every word of this, and I'll be looking for you in the window for a long, long time.

Mister, Your Shoelace is Untied

Picture me, if you feel like it, composing essays not from a desk but a tall breakfast bar, legs swinging from a chocolate leather barstool I hop on, love to hop on, especially if my coffee's perfecto and the sun's rippling through the blinds like hopes and dreams. My day's gotten off to a lovely start. Ahh, the hour, if I'm a lucky girl, is my playground. Except—did I say *composing*? And *essays*? Delete, delete, please delete! Unlike my dad, a voracious reader of philosophy, economics, religion, even the after-life, a scholar to the end, and unlike my scholarly sweetheart who buries himself in dusty archives in Poland and Germany, I don't have an academic bone in my bod, at least not anymore. Like the song goes, school's out—forever! The thought of sitting at a desk by day and writing papers by night . . . shudder. My nephew goes to a high school where they don't believe in sleep; sometimes, I wake up at two a.m. knowing he's at his desk, and it kills me. At the same time, I'm glad I'm not him. Well, I've spent my entire adult life writing my heart out, and now I'm just gonna scribble away, and if the gods are with me, maybe I'll hear a sweet note of gospel while the world trumpets by. If not, oh well. Hey, being a whisper in the woods has its moments. You can hide out with your thoughts. You can find your spot.

I did.

That said, let's go back to the journey from my leather perch and travel with wanderlust, a pretty cool word, I think. I'm also thinking . . . maybe my dad felt guilty leaving his war-ravaged Korea behind, maybe that's why his face looked tentative that farewell day. Whatever his mood boarding the Northwest Orient plane, once he touched ground, his impressions were good ones, that much I know. 1950s America put the spring back in his step; a sense of well-being.

Listen.

Those are black oxfords on white pavement.

After making temporary housing arrangements in Brighton, Massachusetts, for his small family—him, his wife, and toddler daughter Grace—he flew back to San Francisco, the city I'd be named after a year later. "Frances," a name for homely women and grandmothers, isn't the name I would've chosen for myself, and frankly, I still haven't made peace with it, but it beats "Frisco." Anyway, here in San Francisco, he met his just-arrived wife and daughter so he could begin the journey of escorting them to the east coast. From San Francisco, they took a train to Ogden, Utah, and spent some time with an American Army chaplain friend they knew from the American's Korea-stationed days. Next on the itinerary, a plane ride to Chicago where they had a whirlwind visit with Paul Douglass, former president of American University, who was, among other things, an advisor to Syngman Rhee, President of Korea. By whirlwind, think party scene from the film *Sabrina*—crazy extravagant to war-weary Koreans. More culture shock was on display on Lake Shore Drive, where couples smooched in public like it was nobody's business.

Jin jjah ro hah neun geoh ya? Translation: Could it be?

Young wha bo dah naht neh! Translation: This is better than the movies!

After the thrill ride of Chicago, they flew to their ultimate destination, Boston Logan International Airport. My guess is that by now, my dad, with nonstop marvel, was sensing he'd found his place in the world. His spot. I couldn't call it a spot like mine because that would imply stationary, and if ever a fellow was "Par Avion," it was him. Within five years, my dad would be happily sleepwalking through airports and greeting staff by name in hotels on nearly every continent on the globe. Always stopping to smell the roses.

For example, while in Chicago, a little girl had crossed his path and innocently quipped, "Hey, Mister, your shoelace is untied." The young wire-rimmed Korean stopped in his tracks, stunned. Was she talking to *me*? He looked down. Yessiree, his shoelace was untied! God Almighty, here was American liberty, freedom of speech right before his eyes! In Korea, a child would never dream of speaking up like that. This was a good country. Things were getting off on the right foot.

The neighbors on a street called Foster Terrace in suburban Brighton were a tight-knit group. Couples with liberal views populated these modest rowhouses; wives having babies with their grad student

and professor husbands. Overnight, the Korean couple was indoctri-
nated into the 1954 American way of life. My mom was making iced
coffee while my dad was washing a dark blue Ford, their first major
purchase; the two were lighting up Camel cigarettes and going to
Saturday night barbeques. I can see them; I can hear them blending
in—my mom barely spoke a word of English, but laughter sounds the
same in every language. Strange to think the ashes of the Korean War
were still smoking, but what could they do? They were here.

Bet you money it was a beautiful summer evening, a chill in the air.
Rounds of jokes. Ada's got her elbows on her knees, Philip's leaning
back on a lawn chair. My parents' first American friends, the fun-lov-
ing wife and her professor husband, took the younger couple under
their wing. How wonderful. How American. They were Jews, mysterious people my mother grew up hearing if not fearing, a notion
made nonsense with that first knock on the door.

Knock, knock.

The wives, pregnant at the same time, bonded at Foster Terrace
while their husbands went to work. Philip to Boston University,
where he taught experimental psychology; my dad to Harvard, where
he studied for his masters in public administration. Struggled, too. His
Korean ear was trained to interpret conversational English and war
threats against President Rhee, not Harvard profs lecturing from a po-
dium to students who grew up in Connecticut and Ohio classrooms.
That first semester, my poor dad was in his own little foreign hell.
Whenever he saw a particular blinking sign in Cambridge—*Sherman
Bank . . . Sherman Bank . . . Sherman Bank*—a hostile message shot
back at him:

You're going to fail . . .You're going to fail . . .You're going to fail!

Did I come all the way to America just to fail?

A wife, helpless in America, a toddler to feed, a baby coming, an
education in peril. For people who dream big, there are always lonely
moments.Where do you turn? Who is there to talk to? Then, one day,
he heard salvation:

Knock, knock.

It was Philip, offering to help him with his first term paper. Proof-read, check for syntax, clarity. I was never quite sure whether my father, a man of many questions, believed in God, but that day there was light.

Feel free to skip this part, but my mind's reeling to our family's home several years in the future, not our next home, but the one after that. I'm seven, I'm eight, I'm nine, I'm ten, shaggy bowl cut, skinny arms, the same skinny arms typing these words. Even then, I wasn't so gung-ho on real life, not when it took me away from my father's library. Regardless of where I was—even when the family was out for our Sunday drive, and I, head hanging out the window, belted out songs from *South Pacific* like "Some Enchanted Evening" and "I'm Gonna Wash That Man Right Out of My Hair"—I was counting the minutes until I could return there. Curiously, I felt closer to my dad in his library without him than in the car with him, here, where late at night, long after I went to bed, I knew it was just him and his thoughts. Whenever he was overseas, you could find me snooping around, sooner or later coming upon those Harvard reports, which he kept in the bottom drawer of his desk. Pull them out, study the typed papers—blue ink on watermarked onionskin—and always taking note of the grade on the cover sheet, all As and A-minuses, one B-plus. Even then, they seemed old as scrolls.

But back to one bygone night.

"Everyone say 'cheese'!"

I couldn't tell you if I was yet born the night this picture was taken but I do know we would leave Brighton in 1958 when I was three. Memories are spare. Kids passing a poor kitty through pipes that ran between the rowhouses . . . A stooped old lady, so powdery white she seemed dead already, wandering in her garden and offering us treats—candies? cookies?—whenever she saw us. She scared me. I was never sure if she was real or a ghost. To tell you the truth, I still don't. From an upstairs window, watching my dad drive in celebratory circles in the parking lot. Something good happened 'cause he wasn't one to just drive around in circles for no reason. I'm looking down, I see him. A bully named Gary, whom I apparently chased with a broom over a hill to the cheers of Foster Terrace moms. Big balls for a small girl, huh? Not that I remember my finest hour.

Nor do I remember Ada and Philip. I did, however, grow up hearing their names, and the idea of them always warmed me like candles. The kindness of strangers exists. A friend in your corner is restorative. Sherman Bank's sign now blinked:

You're going to succeed . . .You're going to succeed . . .You're going to succeed!

Forty-five years later, I, along with my mom and younger sister, would meet Ada at the Kennedy Center, a planned reunion at a book festival. I could best describe the afternoon as everything wonderful but most of all, full-circle. By then, she and my mom were grandmothers, both their husbands a quarter-century in their graves. Yet I immediately knew who she was when she approached me with a tug on the arm: an old friend.

I love all the faces in this photograph—faces blessed with something you only feel on a night when the moon's high and the sky's sacred and there's that chill in the air. Yeah, those hopes and dreams again. Beyond that, I'd be gleaning fiction, but I do have a few facts under my sleeve.

In the days and years to come, my father would become infatuated more than ever with things Americana, and his loyalty knew no bounds. Take *Reader's Digest*, particularly their "Laughter, the Best Medicine" column. Even when money was tight, he subscribed to *Reader's Digest* because a good chuckle was worth it. He even contributed personal anecdotes, always shrugging like it was just for fun, but I can tell you it would've made his day just to see one tidbit in print. Someday. Well, he never got that happy little note writers live for, but he kept subscribing and kept submitting to the end. I would've thrown the rag in the trash, but people who live through poverty and war don't see things the same way we do.

Sunoco was his gas station of choice, with good reason. As a grad student without an income, Sunoco approved him for a credit card— the first establishment to say *yes* after many *nos* from others. For the rest of his life, given four gas stations at an intersection, he'd steer into Sunoco, and if there was no Sunoco, any gas station but Exxon or Esso (its archaic name). You can figure out why.

And despite his love of Korean food and fine dining during his travels, he engaged in a love affair with American fast food. Watching him dig into a Hardee's burger was to observe a juicy and meaningful relationship take place. I wasn't aware of a favorite but given four fast-food joints at an intersection, he'd choose McDonald's last. Nothing against McDonald's per se; he liked a Big Mac as much as the next guy. But when you're Oriental (another archaic name) in a white world, you always veer toward the underdog.

So now, look at that face, so fresh-faced and handsome, ready to embrace the laughter. This was the face of my father before the hypertension and high blood sugar, before that first demon got to him. Yet, on some enchanted evening in Foster Terrace, in the time it took to smile, he was healthy and happy.

I'd love to leave you with the impression that I dashed this off in one fell swoop from my chocolate leather barstool. That a sunshower just fell and left a rainbow's glow coming through the blinds. Perfect. But life isn't, and I didn't. I actually wrote much of this piece during many stolen moments during a three-week time frame, and except for the opening page, and this final page, rarely was I sitting here. The reality? Like you, I do things. Went on a long road trip with my family so our eighty-three-year-old mom could lay her eyes on Chicago once more; walked along Lake Shore Drive for the first time; its magnificence diminished by regretting that the person who really wanted to see it stayed back at the hotel 'cause her legs can't take it anymore; kissed my sweetheart in the café where we had our first date, and then did something that surprised even myself: I got engaged. Because life does go on. Still, it's comforting—to me, anyway—that on this particular morning as I wrap up this vignette, a perfect word in an imperfect world, I'm back here, at my breakfast bar, on my barstool, as sun ripples through the blinds, remembering my dad.

Nothing Bad Could Happen Here

Oh, what I'd do for a bird's eye view of us cruising down I-95 in our big black boxy Ford, the only Korean family on the road in 1958. At the helm was my dad, looking very Desi Arnaz in those days—the hair minus the cha-cha-cha anyway. He always drove like a man set free and fueled by dreams, probably now more than ever. Diploma in hand, Harvard was history, and a new job at the World Bank was waiting in the wings—*We're staying in America!* By his side was my mom, her left arm forever reaching back to hand me and my big sister treats—ah, the sweet stuff of life: Juicy Fruit gum, butterscotch candies, 7-Ups.

Not that I remember *that* ride, per se. At three, I didn't know north from south the day we moved from Boston to Washington.

Alexandria, actually. Belle View Apartments, precisely.

A sprawling complex over several blocks, Belle View was a maze of brick buildings and courtyards so identical you couldn't distinguish one from another—surely only the postman could find his way out. Apparently, the Potomac River was a stone's throw away, but I never got a sense of water, only grass. Even now, I'm caught off guard when the smell of a freshly-mowed lawn transports me back to the grounds of Belle View not because they were well-manicured but because I was so close to them, knee-high and steeped in grass and dandelion dust, sometimes holding hands with JoAnn, my brown-haired friend. What a beautiful blur of Matisse greens, yellows, whites. It's always spring or summer. Two pretty girls. Nothing bad could happen here.

The Parks' presence became known when rumors began to fly about my dad as if he emigrated from Red China, not South Korea. Well, this was the height of the Cold War era.

"Did you hear? He's a Communist!"

Turned out I was to blame. Someday the story would become amusing family lore, but for now, my parents took me gently aside:

"Don't tell people daddy is a Communist, Frances. Daddy is an *economist*. Understand?"

Through a dreamy lens: our white corner porch that overlooked a pool that, due to my mom's fear of water, I was never allowed near; a magnificent kite-sized yellow monarch butterfly fluttering on the rooftop next to ours, so Felliniesque. Somehow, I got it in my head that it came back to see me every spring. To this day, some forever-young part of me is still looking up and waving.

Hello, butterfly! I'm down here!

In 1960, we left Belle View but stayed in the area, moving into a rambler, then a colonial—east, west, who knows, I never could read a road map or understand what inside or outside the Beltway meant. Then, in 1979, my dad died.

We were lost.

Once in a blue moon, out running errands or driving along the GW Parkway for scenic views of the Potomac, my mom and I would find ourselves near Belle View Apartments. A drive-by, a sigh, that's all; first, it was years, then decades, then half a lifetime ago. Somewhere along the way, a poisonous memory crept back to me like a black widow.

I'll say I was four, but I could've been three or five, wandering around Belle View by myself, as this is what parents let their little kids do back in that mythically safer time. I would go to the playground where two swing sets and seesaws waited for children—odd; it was always so quiet. Or see if JoAnn, who lived in our horseshoe one building over, could come outside and play—*knock, knock.* Or just wander. Most days are fuzzy, but on this particular day, where I stood on the earth—just footsteps from my building's entrance—I can picture like a shoeprint in cement. And from that spot, a gypsy-hiss:

"Frances."

My brain coded her as Rose, a woman who lived in our building but in a basement apartment. Unlike my mom, so young and powdery, Rose seemed old and hardened as a coconut shell.

"Frances, do you like gum?"

"Yes."

Enticingly: "Guess what I have?"

"What?"

"A gumball machine!"

Surely my look of glee was a dead giveaway. Colorful gumballs jumbling around in a glass globe just like the ones in the Spiegel catalog! These were penny-pinching times for my parents, and I whiled away many an hour staring at said catalog, the pages featuring not just gumball but cotton candy and ice-cream-making machines. Dreaming of the day.

"I can show it to you, Frances. Come."

With the promise of a gumball, Rose took my hand. Maybe imagination is lending drama, but stepping down those stairs, I was engulfed in Hitchcock airs, through the dungeon-dark hallway, and into her sunless apartment. But no matter because lo and behold and grand as Oz:

A gumball machine!

"Would you like one?"

"But I don't have a penny . . ."

"Don't worry; you don't need a penny. Just sit in this chair."

The mechanics are a bit fuzzy, but as I remember, Rose placed the tip of my index finger into the lever's coin slot, and before I could process what was happening, she executed her plan with a cruel smile by pushing the lever in and immediately swiping it across the machine. Finger jam-piercing pain-panic paralysis. She repeated her madness until I finally had the four-year-old sense to hop down and run out of there.

Curiously, I didn't tell my parents what happened. Also curious, I have no memory of my mood in the aftermath, or what I did, or how I acted, or whether I ever saw Rose again. Unquestionably, I blacked it out, and if a scar formed, I never saw it. Maybe the idea of someone wanting to hurt me was too awful. Maybe seeing life through a dark lens was too ugly.

Years later, when I did recall the incident, I mentioned it to my mom, by now long-widowed. Had my dad, even dead and buried, learned that his daughter was once lured down to a torture chamber

by a neighbor, he would've come back from the grave and taken re-
venge. But my mom's reaction was flustered, confused, almost as if I
was making up a story. Belle View was a lovely reverie. What neighbor
could I possibly be talking about?

"Her name was Rose," I said. "She lived in the basement. She
might've been foreign."

A composite sketch came together in her head, and she grew sol-
emn. "Not Rose. Her name Blossom."

Blossom?

No matter, she would remain Rose to me.

Apparently, whatever her name was, she was a Panamanian woman married to a much younger master sergeant whom she bragged
about to the other Belle View housewives. The couple had twin boys,
troublemakers, judging by their "cowboy and Indian"-themed birthday party that worked its way outside and got wildly out of hand.
Neighbors talked. After we moved out, my mom heard the family was
kicked out of Belle View.

"Why, Mom?"

"She do something bad."

One warm afternoon in recent history, my mom and I were out
and about, not far from Belle View Apartments. For some reason, she
had an urge to see our old place.

"Park there," she said.

Stepping foot on Belle View grounds for the first time since childhood, I fell into a fog following her through a maze of cloned courtyards and buildings as she roamed around in circles or, rather, squares.
In time, she gave up. Lack of coordinates.

"Can't find."

And then, like dust blown off some ancient map, my head cleared,
and suddenly I knew *exactly* where we were supposed to go: over to
Potomac Avenue where a second-floor corner unit sat perched in
time. As soon as I saw the white porch, one of countless in Belle View,
I felt knee-high again. Rose never crossed my mind.

"That's it, Mom."

"No," she disagreed. "Where is pool?"

Ah. My poor mom had been looking for a by-gone landmark. Once realized, she checked the front of the building to confirm that the address matched the one in her memories.

And it did.

For some reason, I'm tickled by the spirit of that day, when the child-me wandered out of the grownup-me and, like my yellow butterfly, the powers of migration led us to our long-ago home. Horrific things happen to everybody but let me slip into a prism and glorify the Belle View dream, not the nightmare. The monarch, not the monster. The latter can burn in hell.

I See You, I See You

When I see pictures of my late father, I know it's him. And when I see my reflection in a mirror, I know it's me. But even a relatively mild case of prosopagnosia—face blindness—can be a bother. Too often, I don't recognize longtime customers in my sweet shop where we sell bonbons and books, where hanging out is half the fun.

Me: "See you tomorrow!"

Yet I always need a nudge, a memory I can pin to you even though it might not stick, and next time we'll start all over again until one day you walk in, and a bell will go off and suddenly . . .

I see you, I see you. I know who you are.

But one face I thought I'd never forget belonged to a boy from Ohio who came to Virginia Tech to be surrounded by mountains. His name was Henry.

Our story began on a Saturday night in January 1975 when my dorm mate Lulu and I, both sophomores, stumbled into a blues bar called 117 South Main. The honkytonk saloon wasn't a place you'd expect to find me, a girl of Asian descent riddled with insecurities but trying to fit into a rural Virginia college town, not to mention my Levi's. But for some reason, I did. Drinking beer, lots of it, helped.

Then I saw him, leaning over the balcony railing. First the grin. Beautiful. Then the face. Gulp. A certain type, fully loaded, crazy blond, part innocent, part badass, totally irresistible. With a shameless finger, I come-hithered him to me, and he flew down the stairs and the rest that night is forgettable history: I drank too much, made a fool of myself, and who knows how I got back to my dorm. Crawled, probably. The next morning, I vowed to ignore this Henry from Ohio for the rest of my life.

Our paths wouldn't cross again until my senior year. On the eve of fall semester, my roommate Catie and I were walking down Main Street near College Avenue, a corner where a sub shop, a doughnut shop, a head shop, and bars converged. My heart stopped in its tracks: Henry, also with a buddy, was walking on the other side of the street.

"Catie . . ."

Scouting out the situation: "Stay cool, Francie."

Ooh, no can do.

Within the hour, Henry from Ohio and I were splitting a pitcher, and whatever happened to our friends is lost to the ages along with most of the night's conversation except that we laughed about our disastrous meeting of two years ago. Curiously, he said he'd never heard of "quiche" when I said I *looovvved* it, or the word "emaciated" when I called him that. He did say *aw* a lot. Grinning.

"Really, Francie? You're *never* getting married?"

Marriage? The kiss of death. "No."

"Aw, you'll change your mind."

We were ripe for love, you know, having both gone through summer breakups. That said, love never had a chance.

In those days, I was reckless for attention for reasons that had little to do with love: An amped-up ego after dark made me feel like somebody in a white world. Yet Henry's twenty-one-year-old heart, more broken than mine and seemingly unrecoverable from a girl back home, ultimately resisted me, and that drove me to the edge. *Huh?* Did he think I was *nobody?* Too, I'd come to realize his rock 'n' roll hair and lip-perched cigarette were more props than persona—think Opie, not Robert Plant. Desk job-portfolio-wife and kids were on his immediate post-college horizon; he was, after all, from Ohio, and if his family didn't collect Hummels, I'd eat my hat. Meanwhile, I was the mad-about-him demon girl he saw no future with, what with my toxic talk of two a.m. New York subway stories and writing dark novels and acquiring new lovers to my dying day, half of which I said just to blow his Midwestern mind. It all backfired on me, and even when I was in his arms, he held me at bay. Still, the lust was unquenchable, and our conversations in the pitch-black were like bedding: messy and layered.

"What do you *want* from me?" he whined.

"I don't know but, Henry . . ."

"Yeah?"

"Are you glad I'm here?"

"Yes . . . and no."

That aloofness became my drug of choice, my aphrodisiac—not exactly a formula for love. In the end, things got ugly, and when I left Tech, there were no good-byes.

Two years later, my father suffered a fatal stroke, ending life as I knew it. I left my job, put all calls, friendships, and writing dreams on hold, looked after my mom and younger sister. We ended up opening a chocolate boutique so we could stay together and heal together.

In time, memories of Henry from Ohio came back to haunt me, the relationship so unrequited I couldn't get him out of my mind. Sure, I had boyfriends. None could live up to him.

In 1984, seven years after college, I did a most humbling thing: I wrote Henry a letter. A note, really, not a long note, not a love note, just a hello note with telling details: My dad had died; I'd opened a shop. I never heard back—the letter got lost in the mail, or the alumni office gave me an old address, I convinced myself.

Over the next decade, Henry from Ohio went from real person to Henry the Dream, weaving in and out of my thoughts like metallic thread in a gray sky. *I see you, I see you.* That he existed at all seemed like a gift during periods best described as the drudgery of my days. Real life, yawn. Difficult times, no way out. Remembering him was like hearing "Peaceful Easy Feeling" on the radio, bringing back a time before death hit the wall. I could conjure up his face, his grin while driving to work in the rain or drinking coffee in a café and still feel what I once felt. Alive.

More years passed, and I lived my life: writing and publishing books, making media rounds, operating my little shop. I had my circle of friends; I had my lovers. Maybe the calendar was dating me, but the lack of traditional milestones like marriage and motherhood kept me young.

Had Henry from Ohio vanished from my mind's eye? As he might say, yes . . . and no. By now, he was Henry the Myth, someone I'd never see again, never touch again. But there were those humdrum moments when I'd escape back to one moonlit autumn night when we stood in the parking lot across from Squires Student Center about to lock in a kiss so hungry you'd think we'd been starving to death our whole lives.

Did I ever see him again?

Yes.

One unassuming summer afternoon in 2009, his name popped up in my inbox. My poor brain could barely process the subject line: *Time passes quickly said the boy you once called emaciated.* My finger—the same finger that beckoned him to me in a college bar—froze on the keyboard. Dare I open a note I'd been waiting for forever?

Yes.

More than a note, his message was long and heartfelt and eloquent. Above all, apologetic for never replying to my letter of yore, explaining that he'd received it on the very day he returned from his honeymoon and felt guilty. Married now for twenty-five years, he had nothing but praise for his wife. But between the lines, I read misgivings: He said he often thought about me, of us, through the years, and on more than one occasion had called for me at my shop, each time hanging up before I got to the phone. I wrote him back, numbly excited. His next message mentioned the first time he ever laid eyes on me: *So many years have passed, but my synapses are seared with that experience. I'll always remember it as if it happened last week.* True, Henry was married, but life is short, happiness rare, and we were human. After a few exchanges, he wondered if we could meet.

At an appointed Thai café several miles from my home, several hundred from his, I arrived a few minutes before two o'clock and waited in the entrance. Patrons swung through the café doors—no, no, no. So what if years and decades had passed? I'd recognize Henry from Ohio a mile away. Soon, a well-groomed businessman with fair brown hair stood over me. No seventies vibes.

"Francie?"

Logically, I knew who this was, but prosopagnosia set in like a clay mask. Blindly, I searched his face for a trace of recognition.

"Henry?"

Once seated, our shared history took over. His recollection that my father had worked for the World Bank and traveled during much of my childhood confirmed that this person was no imposter. We talked for hours, lost track of time. Then, out of character and out of the blue, he laid his middle-aged heart on a plate:

"I've been tortured all these years, Francie—had you'd written that letter earlier, our lives could've been completely different."

I listened to him bare his soul with those very words over the course of our conversation not once, not twice, but three times until I blurted out:

"Henry, I don't think we would've been happy together."

And just like that, I shut the door on our second chance at love. Sacrificed a thousand longing daydreams. Why? I'll wonder forever. Kick myself forever. But maybe, deep down, I knew it was too late, though I might live out my days tinged with regret.

As we walked down the sidewalk to our respective cars, I looked over at Henry from Ohio when the unexpected happened: His profile in the late afternoon sun struck a familiar silhouette, restoring my vision.

I see you, I see you. I know who you are.

Yet it was time to say good-bye.

"Henry, I might write about this someday."

"You can write *anything* you want."

After we parted ways, Henry rushed back to kiss me on the cheek. The kiss was sweet and desperate, enough to leave an impression. Last us a lifetime. Maybe dreams dim and Levi's fade, but if youth was gone, you'd never know it from our eyes.

A Ghost in Edinburgh

For a reluctant traveler, I felt at home in Edinburgh. And by the time the hired car pulled up to the G&V Hotel, I knew the lay of the land. Me, who feels lost when I step off an elevator. *Right? Left?* Maybe I'd been here before, in a dream, or was still dreaming, looking up at Edinburgh Castle perched atop Castle Rock. Wow. You don't see such sights in the States. On that chilly-for-July morning, maybe our delightful driver, a sturdy Scottish blonde woman, had helped set the tone. I was tired and mute but listening.

"So, are you vacationing in our lovely country?"

"Actually, I'm here for a conference. My wife's keeping me company," my husband said, always eager to engage in light-as-baton banter considering his field and family's background—the Holocaust. Plus, right now, he's a happy traveler who got some sleep on the plane, at least.

"What a shame. You just missed Royal Week."

"Royal Week? When was it?"

"Last week. It was a grand affair," she replied with grand details. "The Queen came for tea, if you will."

"Ah."

Pointing out landmarks, she asked us where we were from. A Jew, an Asian. Could be anywhere.

My husband quipped, "The Washington, DC, area."

Well, I am; most of the time, he's a hundred miles away enlightening young minds about The Third Reich in a sleepy university town.

"Have you visited our nation's capital?" he asked her.

"I have. Wonderful city," she recalled. "But I must say, there was one big disappointment: The White House. I grew up looking at pictures and postcards of this impressive-looking building. But in real life, oh, my goodness, it was so small."

Too early to check in, we left our suitcases—mine, a mess inside; his, arranged neatly as a bento box—at the hotel. To pass the time, we had coffee and croissants in a sweet bakery on Victoria Street. Our room still wasn't ready when we returned, so we waited on a plush sofa in the lobby. While my husband catnapped, the Euro-chatter of privileged young men who hung out in vineyards and brought beautiful girls back to their family apartments in Paris and Rome rang in my ears like echoes from a memory or a foreign film, something I couldn't quite touch until it hit me, right now: my childhood travels, decades and decades ago. Summer, the sixties and seventies. My dad served as the faithful leader of our pack, a Korean family from white America. I loved that, his lead. His worldly stride. I felt safe following him and not safe when he died. Even in my deepest fog, one thing is crystal clear: He deserved his golden years.

These days, my husband, famously late to everything but airports, takes charge.

Edinburgh that first evening cast a gloomy yet invigorating charm. Though I hadn't slept in nearly forty hours, I was able to keep up with my husband and his fellow Jewish academics on a walking tour of storied sites in Old Town. The odd one out, I kept on truckin' even when the rain came; slipped into the shadows and went into ghost-mode as the night wore on. Afterward, a reception in the city's synagogue, then dinner for thirty in an Indian restaurant. Spoke to a soul or two but no soulful exchanges.

Don't get me wrong. I'm no little mouse. I don't take crap, and I drink my coffee black. But I wouldn't argue that *maybe* I carry a ghost gene or two. Deactivate nearly every hotel key I touch; possess an acute ability to sense, even to the day, when people from my past, even my long-ago past, are dead; and, according to TSA's Global Entry Office, have no registerable fingerprints. Also, if nobody's listening, I fade and disappear.

The next afternoon I spent alone roaming up and down the main street known as the Royal Mile—castle on high end, palace on low end—over cobblestones and plaques and under clocks of yore. If you told me I'd been here before, I'd believe you. Half-believe you.

Dotting the steep street were open-gated alleyways crowned with ye olde world nameplates like Real Mary's Close, Advocates Close, Lady Stairs Close, appearing to open up to gothic labyrinths of communal living where Cinderella might've toiled—tenements, courtyards, stairs. In memory, vapors from the plague are seeping out onto Royal Mile. Derived not from the word "closets," as was my educated guess, they were called "closes" because villagers had to close their gates every night to lock out drunks and enemies back in the day. Don't ask me what day; I'm only my own historian.

Like typical tourists, we took in Edinburgh over the next couple of days. Though a homebody at heart, I found it a most charming place, familiar and inviting, full of darling cafes with darling servers. The decors, the simple bistro food, the archaic water jugs, rich coffee in big mugs, love, love, in a light singsong way.

Yet I kept thinking about those closes. The mere idea of them drew me in like a neglected cemetery. On our last day, we decided to step into one, and surprise, surprise, the gates didn't shut behind us as we stood in a courtyard and imagined life back when your neighbor might toss the contents of their chamber pot out the window when you were minding your own business below.

"*Gardyloo!*" my husband shouted, imitating a Scot from the Middle Ages warning passersby to *Watch out for the water!* I'm guessing he read that somewhere.

Departure morning. My husband was chatting with our driver, a sad Scottish gent of fifty or sixty, slight with a crewcut gray as the day and a thick-as-pudding accent. Hours of watching Masterpiece Theatre did us no good here; we found ourselves inching up in our seats to decipher what we could.

"No, sir, I'm sorry to say I haven't been to the States. It's my dream, though. Problem is my wife won't fly."

"Oh," my husband said, feeling for him. I'm no frequent flyer, but at least he can get me on a plane once in a blue moon. "That's a shame."

Our driver nodded. "Yes."

"So," my husband wondered, "how does the life of a driver work? Do you have another job lined up after you drop us off at the airport?"

Whatever his reply, it led our driver to reveal he had to wake up in the wee hours the next morning.

"I'll be driving a client to the seaport. Like my poor wife, she's deathly afraid of planes, so she takes a ship wherever she needs to go. It will be a ten-hour drive to get there."

"Seriously? Ten hours?!"

"Indeed."

"You know, if your wife won't fly, why don't the two of you travel by sea?"

Our driver sighed. "The only thing my wife is more afraid of than planes is water."

OK. Laugh or cry? I mean, it was almost funny. Almost.

"My dream," he said, "has always been to go to the Great Lakes. I love to fish, and I've always wanted to fish there."

I couldn't imagine that dream. Or driving a stranger for ten hours, for that matter. This was a man who'd never known a frill in his life.

At the airport, my husband was figuring out a tip while our driver politely set down our luggage. We said our thank yous and good-byes and turned to go. For some reason, I looked back at him and spoke the only words I clearly remember saying in Scotland:

"Hey, I'm really sorry you have to drive ten hours tomorrow."

We exchanged a genuine moment, the kind of soulful look I live for, even with a stranger I'll never see again who just wanted to go fishing in America. I would say with certainty that his eyes summed up all the long days of his driving life and the dread of tomorrow.

Back home, those closes on Royal Mile came back to haunt me. Behind one of those imaginary mist-ridden gates lay something hidden and buried for me. Not literally but figuratively. Then, my head unlocked.

Lately, before going to bed, I've been tidying up, not a lot, just a little. For me, no neatnik, it's an effort, and I watch myself as if it's not me but someone else. A shadow on a private stage. Gather my shoes from the floor, arrange them neatly in the closet, clear crumpled tissues off the vanity, hang my big pink comb back on the hook. It's so quiet. Meanwhile, a thought pulls me in like a mysterious Edinburgh close whose nameplate has weathered centuries: My dad was younger than me when he died in his sleep. If I don't wake up tomorrow, I don't want to leave this world looking like a slob.

Good-bye, Tess

I wish Tess was with me now, right here on my couch, watching CNN, all fired up, crazy as a cartoon. Tess versus Trump—what a show! Long before we met, she established the first NOW chapter in West Virginia, where she was raising a family with her husband, Jack. Predating that, their front lawn in Charleston was torched for inviting a mixed-race couple over for dinner; the next day, she knocked on doors and gave every neighbor hell. Don't mess with Tess; loving mamas can be fired up liberals, too. Last year, her son Mike posted a video of her, memory mostly gone but values intact, hissing from her wheelchair: "I hate Trump!" In her heyday, she'd be leading the marches. Politics aside, that's not really why I wished she was still here. I just wished I'd said good-bye.

I've always been drawn to older people; who knows why. My dad's parents were demons who put him in an early grave, and even as a little girl, I despised them. My mom's parents were apparently saints, but the Korean War killed off generations of dreams, including theirs, and I never met them. That said, I was always more curious about elders, as if my own generation bored me (or me, them); always wondering about the friend's mother who ironed shirts with a sunny smile, the father who seemed more like a shadow. When I went to Ocean City with two teenaged girlfriends, I ditched them on the beach (seriously, who could lie there all day?) to hang out with their moms. From a convertible, we cruised up and down the main drag, honking away at shocked-looking guys. At dusk, we wolf-whistled at dudes in power-boats from our balcony on the bay, and I gotta say being corrupted by married moms clinking wine coolers was the most fun I had in high school. After college, when I was dating a grad student and obliged to dine at his parents' estate, the only thing that got me through the night was getting drunk with his German grandma who, having hobbled down the stairs as if from some dark tower, lit up whenever she saw me. The home was cold, but she was warm, and I was grateful we could build our little fire, so to say, and drink ourselves silly, though I never understood a word she said. When her grandson and I broke up, I wondered who she would talk to now.

So, in modern times, it made no sense that I never said good-bye to Tess. My emotions for this outspoken feminist who lived through the Depression without a mother, whose Irish wit—her *Tessisms*—zinged by me so fast I never caught a single one and was left dumb, ran so deep that frankly, it was preternatural, and if I tried to figure out why, I'd fail because some things aren't meant to be dissected and analyzed, only whittled down to this: She was my friend.

I own a sweet shop, and for the past five years, at any given moment on any given day, whether I was helping a customer hand-pick a box of assorted chocolates or filling up on cocoa-dusted confections, I was also contemplating making the two-hundred-mile drive from the DC suburbs to the Mapleshire nursing home in Morgantown, West Virginia, to see Tess one last time. A couple of times a year, I'd ask our manager to make a day trip with me, and he always said he would because he knows my history inside and out.

So, the thought was there, always there. *Go see Tess, go see Tess.* And yet, I never did.

Like some exotic bird, she flew into my life one lunch hour in 1987, more spirited than your average Washington, DC customer in the middle of a workday. Later, I'd learn that was just her style, along with shawls and hats. Avant-garde.

"One Grand Marnier truffle, please! I've tried them all, but these are my favorites. Must be the booze! It's the Irish in me! The chocolate-covered apricots are my second favorites—I could eat that whole tray, but I only allow myself one a day!"

Judging by her entrance, she'd been in the shop before, and maybe we'd even spoken before, but that day, she was hell-bent on making her presence known. *Tess is here!* I recall the moment so vividly that I'm still there, behind the counter, wondering whether this woman with the bouffant platinum hair was an aging starlet or a lady-of-leisure who came downtown once a week to get her hair done at

Norbert's Salon downstairs. Neither was her story.

Her story was a glorious patchwork of ragged, tragic, and trium-
phant scraps. In the fifties, she married Jack in Springfield, Massachusetts, and the couple moved to Charleston, West Virginia, for his job
with the phone company. In the sixties—because it's hard to keep a
Tess down, even after four kids—she went to work, first in the State
Senate and then their Supreme Court. Following a crushing divorce
through no fault of her own, she left everything behind, even furniture she would later pine for, to start life over in the DC area where
she didn't know a soul. Her decision was gutsy, rash, a madwoman
dash, but at least it brought sixty-year-old Tess to a world of politics,
art, and culture, which she could (sort of) see from a book-cramped
apartment that (sort of) overlooked the Potomac River. And that's
where our story began.

In age and optics, we were night and day. Yet together we were
that perfect moment at dusk. She knew that I, having lost my dad
too young, had a hole in my heart and walked on the spiritual side
of things; I knew that she, despite her fierce fight for equal rights,
yearned for those days as a wife and a mama. She knew I had an
oft-reckless love life; I knew she was still in love with Jack. That aside,
the attraction of souls is a mystery. Cosmic. How many times on the
phone or over decadent little cream-filled pastries from Sutton Place
Gourmet did we declare that we could count our friends on one
hand?
A thousand times, it meant everything.

In the late nineties, Tess took a bad fall in her bedroom, shattering
her hip and leg. In a way, that was the beginning of the end. My dy-
namo was down and would never regain her free-spirited step—the
neighborhood's cobblestone streets made life hell for an old goddess
with a cane. Before too long, Tess told me she was returning home to
West Virginia.

God no. Leaving furniture behind was one thing, but the world you love? Plus . . . I didn't want her to go.

"I need to be near my kids, Frances."

And Tess was gone. First to Charleston, then to Morgantown. The years to come would prove trying, punctuated by the unimaginable loss of her daughter Bridget to breast cancer; a romance out of no-where (an infatuated widower wormed his way into her life; wined, dined, even proposed to her before showing his true colors: rich rac-ist); and, finally, declining health.

When I said Tess was spirited, I meant like Jack Daniels, not in a spiritual sense. She, a self-proclaimed recovering Catholic, never came off as even remotely religious. But then she began attending occasion-al Mass. It was so un-Tess.

"Now that I'm almost there, Frances, I gotta cover all my bases."

I once asked Tess a question that was probably voodoo to her ears: If she *did* die, and if she *could*, would she leave me signs, so I would know she was still here? Make something appear out-of-the-blue? They could be feathers or pennies but placed unexpectedly. Her choice.

Mystical talk baffled Tess and her reply was a bit absent. "Oh, I don't know . . . oranges?"

Oranges—noted. It never came up again.

As time passed, communication got tricky. Her memory was fad-ing, and she was often confused. Halfway through one call, I realized she thought I was someone else. Telling her I got married was a new announcement every time. Sometimes she'd insist her phone number had changed, then grow exhausted and hang up before I could ex-plain otherwise. For months I couldn't get through to her and feared the worst. One morning, she finally did pick up, frazzled.

"Frances, I'm in a hospital! I'm ready to go home now, but they won't let me out!"

Luckily, her son Mike was by her side. He explained to me that Tess wasn't in a hospital but in a nursing home, for good.

Go see Tess, go see Tess. The mere thought made me spasm from some deep, skeletal fear. Once I said good-bye, it was over. Mike and I promptly became Facebook friends, and his daily posts helped keep the Tess-dream alive.

She's still here!

Still smiling!

Two weeks ago, a Wednesday, he sent me a half-minute video of Tess, frail but alert. After thanking me for the Easter chocolates, she recounted how she used to come into the shop every day for her bonbon du jour, then expressed her love. I teared up.

Bye-bye, Frances, were her last words.

I put it on my calendar to call Tess the following week, Friday, in fact. But Wednesday morning, she was near death. There were close calls before, but this was it. At 9:40 a.m., shaking so bad I could barely text, I asked Mike, if possible, to let his mom know how much I loved her. Yet, the minute my text dinged him, Tess passed away. No good-byes.

The following day, I was reading a story from my new copy of *The Massachusetts Review,* which opens up with the narrator's dead mom, a ghost, arriving at his table in Berlin with a bag of oranges. Nothing hit me until hours later, and I flipped back to the story, to the title page: *Oranges.* A ghost. With oranges. A coincidence, I'm sure. Just one of those things. Yet I like to connect dots; some might even say I connect dots and create constellations that aren't there. But that's how I make sense of my universe.

Oh, I almost forgot to mention something: I did visit Tess once, in Charleston. It was 2004, give or take a year. She met me at the airport, aged and puffier than before. Walking was still a nightmare for her, but she drove us to her place like she owned the West Virginia mountainside.

Cruised!

That night, I crashed on her couch. Her bedroom door was ajar, and in the dark, I became aware of her presence like a nearby candle. There she is. Aglow. Burning. I'm not sure if I heard Tess breathing or just thought I did, but the hole in my heart filled up. Maybe that was our good-bye.

Serving God, Meat, and Intercourse in an Amish Diner

Ziggy Stardust and Southern Boogie dominated the FM airwaves the era I lived on greasy tacos from Jack in the Box, ditched high school cap and gown for the beach, wrote poetry and drank vodka-laced Tab, and was in love with two boys who were best friends, all the while struttin' around with an ego I'd slap today. I was at an age when you think life is more than it is, and every hour is journal-worthy. I had dreams, you know, and they weren't to grow up and be a mere whistle in the woods.

Now I'm in an Amish-owned restaurant off a country road in Lancaster County, Pennsylvania, with my eighty-two-year-old Korean mother.

The vibes were good here, though. Quiet. We stumbled in at an off-hour for an early dinner as we were already out and about, and I was anxious to get back to our hotel room and call it a day. Our road trip every autumn is sacred on a plane where more, *many* more, lie ahead on our horizon, but, funny thing, I'm a poor traveler, no sense of direction, easily frazzled and sometimes so busy measuring the earth's bitch-o-meter I forget to live. My mom survived the Korean War and doesn't give a damn.

"Someone don't like me, I say, *Puh, I don't like you!*"

After a greeting, a hostess takes us to a table by a window. A sunny waitress hands us menus. Grayish-blonde gals, if they don't like us, they don't show it. Like every baby boomer, I think I look young for my age, but maybe the real world, or at least rural Pennsylvania, sees us as two aging Orientals.

"Welcome, ladies. What can I get you to drink?"

For the record, I'm no frumpy Aunt Bee in big pants or Korean *halmoni* with a bad perm, aggressively steering a grocery cart in Lotte. I still look good in jeans and write my heart out like it'll beat forever. Once in a blue moon, even dot on sparkly eye stuff and wanna go dancing even when there's nowhere to go. I'm no granny in any language.

That said, walking on the wild side means coffee after three o'clock these days.

"Coffee and water, please," I say.

To me, not the waitress, my mom orders, "Same thing."

She's always been a funny bird but, lately, curious little changes mark our days.

Like her crooked pictures. Last fall, we visited Shepherdstown, a village of zombies, though maybe the normal people stayed indoors that day—a bust if not for the backdrop of West Virginia. When my mom snapped a pic of me leaning against our balcony in the Bavarian Inn, she captured it like a stoned flamingo: the Potomac River Bend, the mountainside, a sweeping bridge—just not my head. *Headless in Hickville*, the postcard would read.

And her vanishing acts. At check-out lines in Safeway or H-Mart, while we're loading coffee and oatmeal or seaweed sheets and Asian pears onto the conveyer belt, she'll inevitably rethink her shopping list and disappear down an aisle.

Mom?

The waitress sets down our beverages, too spirited to be Amish, in my opinion, but if she doesn't come from a long line of moonshiners, I'll eat my hat. Or bonnet.

"You ladies ready to order?"

A lifetime ago, after a breakup so bad I needed every molecule in me changed and re-arranged, I gave up meat. Men and liquor, too, but that didn't last.

"I'll have a garden salad, coleslaw, and green beans," I reply. "And a biscuit."

Her expression says it all. *Where's the beef?*

"Meatloaf with that?" she asks.

The scene about to unfold amuses my mom, her face comically decapitating. *I'm a barbarian*, she loves to gloat, just to get my goat. Yup, a carnivore to the core, vegetarians kind of irk her, even when they're good daughters innocently cobbling together a meal from a meat-on-meat menu.

"No ..." I reply.

"Chicken pot pie? Baked ham?"

"No ..."

"Giblet gravy over the biscuit?"

"No ..."

God, no!

Growing up, sometimes I found myself trying not to think about the dead thing on my plate, the braised Korean short rib or barbequed chicken wing that couldn't be mistaken for anything other than something that could fly off the plate. Boned-in things. Fish sticks, hotdogs, and hamburgers weren't usually a problem, but rows of fine blond hairs on drumsticks about to hit the grill, illuminated in sunlight, could kill any illusion.

"Are those *hairs*, Dad?"

He could always cook up a simple, good response. "Not if you don't look at them, Fran."

Giving up on me, the waitress turns to my mom, chicken-less these days since her acupuncturist Dr. Kang says certain foods like fowl and apples and oranges can affect her balance, and we don't need no stinking drumstick messing with her yin and yang. Turning to me, she licks her chops and orders.

"Fried fish platter, Miss!"

Nursing her coffee, my mom takes in the pastoral décor and wonders: "What Amish food, exactly?"

Beats me. "Old-fashioned and fresh is my guess."

She murmurs while I glance out the window.

Holy trinity.

Under threatening skies is a vision straight out of a Coen brothers film: Mounted on tall poles sticking out of grassy grounds like movie props stand three larger-than-life billboards.

Billboard #1, in the image of an open bible: *Believe only the Lord JESUS CHRIST and Thou Shalt Be Saved..Acts 16:31*

Billboard #2: *Award-winning Meats Since 1954. Stoltzfus Meats. Home of the Famous Stoltzfus Country Sausage. Intercourse, PA. Three Miles Ahead on Right.*

Billboard #3: *Stoltzfus Farm Restaurant. All You Can Eat For One Price!*

God, all the meat you can eat, and an Amish town named Intercourse. To my unabashed snicker, my mom peers out as if decrypting code.

"What so funny?"

Bless her Korean heart. Daughter of missionaries, now a grandma cast in hour-long prayers every night—lips moving, no sound—not to mention a lover of Costco's pepperoni pizza, the view doesn't amuse her, though a certain double entendre likely goes over her head. I happen to believe every woman should leave a trail of lovers behind; my God, even Dorothy from *The Golden Girls* had at least four lovers during its run. But a once-virgin bride who still thinks and dreams in Korean might miss the humor, much less the saying about two Amish towns: *The road to Paradise passes through Intercourse.* An hour ago, while driving the stretch of Lancaster County, we stopped in Intercourse, and everything was charming, tame as an Amish orgasm, except for me and the smirk on my face. We walked around and posed for pics. She in front of Pappy's Kettle Korn Shoppe, me in front of Kitchen Kettle.

"Higher, Mom! Point the camera higher!" I was yelling to heaven because a camera in her hands means only one thing: a requiem for my beheading.

"Up, up!"

Click!

On second thought, maybe her lack of frame and aim isn't an age thing. Maybe it's the way she's always seen the world. Somewhat skewed.

A half-century ago, my globetrotting parents took him-and-her snapshots of each other posing on some magnificently marbled plaza in Europe, probably Rome or Athens. Back in the US, the developed film came back from People's Drugstore revealing a funny if not futuristic composition: His picture of her was perfectly centered while hers of him was as tilted as the Leaning Tower of Pisa. Half my dad's head was missing, too.

Considering the off-on drizzle, the day turned out a success, if you ask me. Eight hours earlier, I had my doubts when our horse and buggy tour was canceled due to morning rain, and I was, oh God, oh God. My mom didn't come to Pennsylvania Dutch Country without seeing what it's all about.

Disappointed, she'd plopped on the hotel bed, and, with that, I recalled something she once uttered under her breath in a tone so guttural, so tribal, it sounded like someone else, or the part of her buried beneath her bones, unearthed only in the most broken moment of widowhood. *Daddy gone so long, I don't remember have husband.* In the early years after our loss, I would drive over after work to share supper and talk brave while I hardened like a corpse, only to go home half-drunk on jug wine, half-praying a drunker driver would hit me head-on. *Smash me into a million windshield scattered bits* is what I scribbled in my journal one late night in 1980. I wouldn't go to hell for such thoughts because I lacked the DNA to believe in hell, then, now, and even when I was a twelve-year-old know-it-all furiously penning a letter to Reverend Billy Graham. After watching one of his televised crusades, here was my big, burning question: How can someone repent for sins they don't even *remember* committing? You're asking me to do that, right? Fake repent? Well, forget it! His disciples wrote me back a letter that ended: *We'll pray for you, Frances.*

Did they really pray for me? And if so, for how long? A minute, at most? And it must've been a hollow prayer fanned out to the masses, dismissive as dust, because their God, imagined or otherwise, took away the only person I would've sold my soul for.

January 1978. I begged him not to, but he got up at four a.m. the morning my girlfriends Robin and Kim and I were moving from the quiet DC suburbs to the Big Apple. *New York, New York*, Sinatra would sing the following year. I was hungry to make a name for myself in the East Village as, what else, a boho poet. The East Village sounded like a cool place, and I bet I could rock the look: black glitter tees, skin-tight jeans. I could live and die in that look.

Unlike Robin's dear dad, a big, rugged trucker of a man, mine was a diminutive scholar, and I didn't want him hauling furniture into a van—he wasn't made for that. I didn't want to say good-bye because sometimes a good-bye can feel like a prelude to death. But there he was, there he is, we're driving off, and he's standing in the twinkling blackness like the only soul in the universe, not part of the moving party but wishing he was, forever crowned by stars as one arm shot up like a missile, *Good-bye, Fran.* Robin's dad would live well into the millennium, but mine would only celebrate one more New Year's.

The East Village of that era was hell on earth. Godless. To this day, the smell of new paint, not any paint but some cheap industrial paint used to recoat underground parking garages, brings me back to that $300 a month railroad apartment on East 5th Street where the floors were mud-packed, the fixtures grimy, and cockroaches fell from the ceiling. I can still hear Kim, rudely awoken in the middle of the night by a critter crawling on her face, her screaming, *I just want a warm body next to me! I just want someone to fuck me! I hate it here!*

Not exactly my scene, either.

Outside our door was a nightmare of so many punk rockers you'd think we were the freaks. At the entrance to our walk-up, brash Puerto Rican boys blew dope smoke in our face for kicks like we were virgins from the sticks. In a way, we were because we'd never seen parading transvestites before. Granted, Ukrainian peasants milled quietly about in the background, minding their own business, and on the corner was The Binibon, an all-night café that I came to see as candlelight in rubble, a sanctuary for a civilized cup of coffee, though a couple of years later, it would become the infamous spot where

Norman Mailer's protégé prisoner pal murdered a waiter.

I tried to stick it out, but I don't remember a single moment of sunshine, just steel, suicidal skies. Boho poets have to pay the rent, but anything I hoped for, thought was mine, fell through.

My hometown friend Jack called to see if he could come to visit. I told him:

"Sure, just bring your truck."

For a guy who looked like Warren Beatty, he was an innocent. Too sweet for New York. When the Puerto Rican boys wrote GO HOME on his grit-covered truck, he just shrugged and said:

"Life in the big city, huh?"

That weekend we all partied, went to The Binibon, ran through Washington Square at three in the morning, and saw the Statue of Liberty. Monday morning, I said:

"Pack my shit, Jack. I'm going back with you."

Once home, I did what we all do more than once, like it or not: replaced one life with another. With two other girlfriends, Catie and Patti, I rented an apartment in a section of Arlington, Virginia, known as Rosslyn, just before the Key Bridge. The unit had panoramic views of water and bridges and monuments that canceled out the unrenovated kitchen, the occasional cockroach, and nightly false fire alarms. One look and my dad's spirits sank for me; the twenty-two-year-old daughter he wished was married by now and deep into a novel that would change the world. *This is how my Fran lives?* One night after work, hoping to spruce up the apartment, he showed up at the door balancing a grand oval mirror nearly as tall as him. On our dingy walls, it was a jewel among junk. My dad wanted more for me, not a palace, just an idyllic little cottage with a desk that overlooked a garden of azaleas where I could write in peace.

Not long ago, I revised what God, if there is a God, was trying to tell me during my East Village disaster of 1978: *Your father is going to die soon. Go home and take care of your mother.*

"Day ruined," my mom moaned. No Amish adventure? "What we are to do?"

No, no, no, the day is not ruined. No heart procedure or broken hip surgery could keep us down for long, and now a little rain ain't gonna rain on our Amish parade. Through the years, my love life luminous or dull, I've taken on the role of her husband—shopping partner, dining out partner, road trip partner—and the chances of me leaving her are about as likely as me running off with an Elvis impersonator. Besides, we still have more road trips ahead of us. Many more.

Hallelujah! A hotel pamphlet in the room advertised ninety-minute bus tours departing from the Visitors Center, a stone's throw from the hotel. If not for the rain and my mom's hip, we could walk.

The center was run by two retired farmer types eager to assist anyone who came through the door. Bless their hearts. They weren't strangers who stared or rednecks who glared; they were a different form of life than Miss H, who had wished I was dead or at least not a student in her second-grade classroom. "Your bus leaves in twenty minutes, young ladies."

"Complimentary coffee right over there."

I could wait here forever. I could call this home. Comfy sofa. Huge rural mural painted in warm colors of orange and green. Gents in overalls and a coffee station to boot. Hostile temp, zero.

On a Plexiglas plate, my mom's fried fish platter arrives with all the fixings. Hushpuppies, coleslaw, sauces galore in tiny tin cups. Moon-sized onion rings. My plate arrives as an afterthought. I can almost hear my brother-in-law, who seems to think I live on bowls of oats, seeds, and sprouts, once again quip:

Now that's a meal any bird would be proud to eat!

In a husky voice that, like her prayers, is part of her daily declaration, my mom begs me to "Eat meat!"

My sad little wilted garden of a meal makes no sense to someone who's known war and starvation. Meat will always remain a delicacy, even if we're talking about tacos from Jack in the Box.

She digs in; I dig in. The thought of dead animals in my digestive tract, much less an all-you-can-eat meat buffet, will always make me ill, but watching her feast is a high-fiver. For so long after her hip surgery, she looked grave-ready. Pain meds, you know. Murdered her appetite.

The night before both her operations, I prayed to anyone listening. It takes balls to say you don't believe in God, so I won't, even though the ghost of me knows.

I'm guessing my dad had his doubts but kept them hushed between the pages of books about the afterlife and prophecy, some hokey, some not, an odd collection on his bookshelves considering his more intellectual tastes. Books by Bishop James Pike, Jeanne Dixon, etc. I remember paging through them, along with his scrawls in the margins. I'd call his questioning more open-minded than faithless.

I'm glad my mom has her faith intact, not just in her darkest hour but all hours. It serves her well, and I bow to that. Though I do wince when Facebook posts like this pop up: *Heaven is a place where all the dogs you ever loved come to greet you.* Really? Seriously? Like hell, heaven's a hard place for me to fathom. No coffee, I take it. No wine or chocolate, either, I'm sure. But dogs, you say? I've loved three in my lifetime, and sure as menopause ain't no keg party, no doggies will be waiting for me in heaven. Not even my dad will be there. And, believe me, he would if he could.

My younger siblings Sam and Ginger were in their teens, just babies, too young, too young, the night a relative gathered us in my parents' rec room to break the news: En route to Seoul with my mom, in the Hyatt Regency Waikiki, our dad died in his sleep. Closed his eyes and did what he did not, did not, did not, want to do: leave us. A horribly Disneyesque scene followed—my little brother and sister turned to stone, statues that would crack in time, while I grabbed my brother's waist and screamed like there was no tomorrow, and in a way, there wasn't.

Looking back, I was not a big sister that night. I could only think of my loss, not theirs, not even my mother's, as she withered on the ninth floor of a hotel room in Honolulu.

Our tour bus guide was cut from the same cloth as the sweet old dudes in the Visitors Center, if not slightly frayed at the edges. He was on a schedule, after all, and the group, mostly middle-aged couples from the heartland, was moving like cattle on Quaaludes.

"Come on, come on, folks, the land of the Amish is waiting," he said, ushering everyone onto the bus. When he spotted my mom, the elder, his face softened. Twinkled is a better word. "You take your time, ma'am."

We took our seats, and I couldn't be happier. Blissful. For ninety whole minutes, someone else would be in charge.

The guide was giving it his all. *It* being a labor of love as he drove us through farmland in a spotty rain and explained the Amish way of life, though I was only half-listening because I was only half-interested—my bad, but I tend to lump Amish, Mennonites, Mormons, Muslims, Puritans, and Hindus together in a religious stew of people who can never drink wine with dinner. I can't help it. My mom, on the other hand, was straining to make out every word the guide said, soaking up garbled syllables through lousy acoustics. Rain and a shoddy microphone.

Apparently an Amish insider, the guide was up-to-date on all the current events around these parts—health, welfare, weddings, even what went on behind closed farmhouse doors. Yes, gossip exists in Goody-Two-Shoes Land.

"Even Amish husbands lose their way, folks," he said, offering up a couple of juicy but vague details. "Broke up that household."

So they *do* have intercourse in Intercourse. Moments in the dark, too.

We've all been in the darkness where suddenly, atomically, the room shifts, and who you are in the light of day—the Gidget or Gilligan in you, grinning on the elevator—flies out the window. But this, this is the real you, breathing like some wild animal in wait, stripped down to nothing and everything.

Room One. I was so mad for a boy named R, I thought I'd lost my mind and gladly, gratefully, like I feared you couldn't be a free spirit forever. He wasn't my first lover, but compared to R, the others were squirts. Forgive the pun—as with him, I couldn't resist. He was, of course, a bad boy not for the faint of heart and wickedly good at holding a palette or a girl in his bed in a garden apartment. Watching him over me doing his thing as moonlight and moving headlights slipped through the Venetian blinds was sheer cinema. What a show, with me perfectly content to play the voyeur, mentally taking notes, filming. His hair was a mane, and when he tossed his head back like a sweet hungry beast singing "Golden Lady," I knew I'd have this reel forever, something to lust over when I was a dried-up old lady.

Room Two. Many years later, I was someone else, going through that period when I gave up meat, men, and liquor. You could put Colin Firth's Mr. Darcy in front of me, and nothing would register. I was that half-dead. Sparkless. The thought of a man in my arms was as far removed as the moon over R's bedroom so long ago. That girl never existed. Not in this realm. One night, alone in bed, I heard the sounds of a couple making love in a nearby apartment coming through the walls. They amplified the room to a feverish pitch. For what seemed like hours when it was probably minutes, the woman moaned. I never felt so hollow. Everyone was alive but me.

Late October, harvest season over, few signs of Amish life dotted the fields and farms, a man on a tractor here, a woman tending a garden there, and I felt a bit like a voyeur, again, staring out.

"Before we head back, we'll stop at an Amish country store. Fifteen minutes tops, folks. Please show these wonderful people how much you appreciate their hospitality. They opened up their land and lives to you, so be good sports and open up your wallets to them."

The size of a 7-Eleven, the store was jammed with freshly baked breads and pound cakes, glassware, pottery, Christmas candles, etc. With her usual enchantment, my mom wandered up and down aisles where everything was a novelty, including the lovely bonneted girls who worked there. Polite but Amish to the bone, they shunned any down-to-earth exchange.

Last in line, my mom purchased two loaves of sourdough bread and two quilted potholders with royal blue trim. In no hurry, she began second-guessing herself. Did she want the salt and pepper shakers? Exchange the potholders for the oven mitts? She rarely walks out of a store in a straight line, but I could hear the tour bus, its motor running. Another bus rolling in meant our time was up. I took her arm.

"Let's go."

As our bus began to move, my mom glanced back at the country store, already growing nostalgic for all the Amish knickknacks she left behind.

There's a bigger story here, raw and poignant, about how she lost everything in the war, including the mother and home she left behind in what is now North Korea. So, when a line began to form outside a pretzel booth window, she blinked. Nearly panicked.

"Why they are there?"

"To buy something; that's all, Mom."

She squinted. "What they are buying?"

"Hot pretzels. Just like the ones in the mall. No big deal."

Oh, but it was a big deal. These weren't mall pretzels, and even if they tasted exactly like mall pretzels, it didn't matter.

"Mister! Listen, Mister, stop bus!"

And he did.

The bus waited while my mom took her time coaxing her pretzel out of its waxy bag. Just the top. Just a bite. Her face swooned like it was chocolate or something.

"Taste, Frances. *Authentic* Amish pretzel."

Amish Schmamish; a pretzel was a pretzel. But if it meant getting this show on the road, I'd swallow it whole.

My bite, more a nibble, was still warm and buttery and better than any mall pretzel, sprinkled with grains of salt so perfectly placed the poet in me wants to say God lent a hand.

True, the waitress is probably a bingo-playing grandma who's aware we're barely the same species, but, hey, we're all women of a certain unsexy age, and we're all in the same boat, just trying to live our lives. Within the confines of this Amish-owned diner, she's been good, giving us our space even as she clears the table.

"Anything else, ladies? Dessert? More coffee?"

"Just the check," I say, "thank you."

"Thank you," my mom repeats.

Her meal, she remarks to me, was delicious, though her rating is based on a Pennsylvania Dutch Country scale. Naturally, she'd rather eat Asian any day of the week, but she was here for the Amish experience.

My meal was so-so, but my view? Unscripted and glorious. I had dreams, you know, back when every hour was journal-worthy. But today, a billboard trilogy under atmospheric skies will have to do. I take a pic, imagining the wacky photograph my mom might snap—of headless poles sticking out of God's earth.

A Historic Pause

Every family has its famous photos, as did ours, and all my life, a black and white image—not a playful caricature but a postwar portrait from years earlier, 1954, to be exact—has floated in my head like a leaf or a petal or a ghost from a dream half-forgotten. A young man is boarding a Northwest Orient jet. He looks happy, not jubilant. The hat, well, it's a nice touch but his bon voyage is a bit lackluster, isn't it? Maybe he's tired, not quite his crisp self. Gray skies will do that; wear a man out and make him look like he's at journey's end before the plane's even taken off. But . . . hmm. What about his eyes? Where are the sparks? You'd expect sparks in the face of a dream coming true back when dreams were bigger and meant something. From here, six decades later, I can't see any, but then I wasn't there. Maybe they're muted like stars on a cloudy night.

Besides, what can you really draw from a picture?

A quarter-century later:
Even then, the night he called me, I wondered.
It's true that no one could steal a leisurely moment on the gold brocade-covered couch in the living room like him. Smoke a cigar with slo-mo love, or sip a Scotch on the rocks, exhausted to ashes. Living it up in the 'burbs! TGIF, he loved to enunciate on Friday nights like a typical American dad, not that he was, not by a longshot. Come sit with me, Fran. His shoulders would soften like candle wax. I want you to do great things with your life. Become a teacher or a scientist—do you know how proud that would make me? Use your brain. Be wise. Don't think about money. Read philosophy! There was a fellow, his name was Augustine, who left the material world behind and spent his life seeking light. Granted, Fran, not the light I would follow, but that is not the point I am trying to make: He knew who he was. If you waste your time listening to too much rock 'n' roll music, you will never know who you are. Understand, Fran?

TGIF aside, no matter where he was, his modus operandi was work, in the office, in the garden, on a Northwest Orient flight over the South Pacific Ocean. This I heard through the family grapevine: During the blizzard of 1979 when all of DC was paralyzed, he left our green-shuttered yellow house on a hill, and in fine Dr. Zhivago form, braved his way up our street and over Rolling Road to the Metro stop to wait for a bus that never came. I can picture him right now, a solitary figure in a snowy mess, his eyeglasses frosted, hope dimming on a day so many winters ago. Where is the bus? No bus meant a day hunched over his desk in the den, a garage-converted room so cold you could see your breath, where the red coils of a coal-black space heater struggled in vain, and a TV blared from the rec room. Daytime television—what is this nonsense?—confounded him to no end, but kids were kids, and he didn't want to yell. Like so much in the world, in the end, it would only break his heart . . . Where is the bus? At some point, the Ivy League-educated father of four gave up and trudged back home.

Focus…click! My dad, in character.

But not the night he called me. Flying home the next day, I'd been visiting a guy up north who'd taken me to Toronto, where we partied day and night for a straight week. Poor Dad. The daughter he thought was most like him, a bookworm at birth, the daughter he pictured in laboratories and libraries, not nightclubs, the daughter he wrote deeply reflective letters to from four corners of the globe, had different ideas these days. I wasn't a living nightmare, but I wasn't the Fran of his dreams anymore, either.

On the phone:

"Fran?"

For the record, he was the only person on earth who could call me "Fran" and get away with it. I liked the way he said it, like a well-heeled Brit, not some Virginia hick. As a student, he'd taught himself English from a British dictionary, phonetics, expressions, and all; now, every word that sprang from his lips made everyone else sound like a jailbird.

"I will pick you up from the airport tomorrow."

"My flight's coming in at noon, Dad, in the middle of the day."

Workaholics don't take off in the middle of the day, in the middle of meetings and report-writing and whatever else he did at the World Bank.

"I am taking off."

"From *work?*"

"Yah."

"The whole day?"

"Yah."

Yah? The apartment I rented in Arlington was just a couple of miles from National Airport, as it was known back then. I could hop on the subway or take a taxi, no big deal. Plus, my dad had a long list of loose ends to tie up before leaving in a few days on a six-week World Bank mission to Korea, my mom in tow. He always did. True, airports were his second home. But take the whole day off? That'd be a first.

"You don't have to do that, Dad. I'll just grab a cab."

He protested. "I will be there."

"Fran! Over here!"

As far as I could tell from my visits overseas, Korean men of his generation on the streets of Seoul universally stood diminutively at five-foot-four with either very bony or very boxy builds depending on their luck after the war. Despite my observation, which I took to be fact, my dad felt cheated out of a couple of inches. Fran, my family slept in one room, on the floor, mother, father, brothers, sisters, all cramped together. You could barely move or breathe. If I just could have stretched my legs, I would be five feet five, maybe five feet six …Why didn't you just go to another room, Dad? What other room, Fran? You think we lived in a palace? Our home was just one room! His theory aside, as a child, I remember wishing he was as tall as the other dads, or at least not the shortest dad wherever we went, to High's Dairy or Sears or the carnival. But unlike a house that wasn't really perched on a hill just slightly higher ground, a mound, really, a home we coded as more elevated and therefore more majestic than our neighbors', in time, I would come to see that my father really did stand tall. Stood out. His hair, still black as a magic marker, was combed back to expose a sunny if not scholarly glow. His shirt, a splashy number from the Philippines, pale yellow linen with embroidered white flowers was a good look on a thinker with a boxy build. But the truth was, it was just him. In a sea of people, he towered.

"I see you, Dad!"

I see you, Dad; you were there that day...

After our traditional airport greeting—a quick peck on the lips— he took my bags and led me out of the airport.

"Wait here, Fran, while I get the car."

"I'll go with you."

"No, you are tired."

From a one-hour flight? I can barely walk in high heels today, but in 1979, two years out of college, I could run in them. Besides, the airport was hardly the monstrosity it is today; the satellite parking lot right there, in view. Still:

"You rest," he said, seemingly hell-bent on me not lifting a finger.

And he was off.

There he is, rushing through the parking lot, growing smaller and smaller, leaving me behind. In my archives, he's always in and out of airports, a restless traveler coming and going, looking for The Dream, a place to find peace of mind, an elusive thumbtack on the map between poverty and paradise, a deep place he was never going to find.

In the dark green Torino, my dad's Old Spice filled the car. Old Spice, nice. It occurs to me as I write this that Duncan Hines Spice Cake was my dad's favorite, which explains why the aroma of Old Spice aftershave or spice cake in the oven meant he was around or coming around—it wasn't something we took for granted. At the wheel:

"Fran?"

"Yes?"

"I had my annual physical yesterday."

From his history, my heart pinched. "Yeah?"

Despite a brisk walk and youthful for fifty-six, my father was far from the picture of health. There were scares, not many but enough. One long-ago night that felt like midnight, I looked up at a hospital window from my bus seat and caught his silhouette, a haunting sight in the window of a room so high up I felt hollow as an orphan as the bus pulled away; I waved, and he waved back; he saw me, yes, I'm sure he saw me. Just yesterday, I asked my mom about this memory; she told me we were leaving Washington Hospital Center, and the year was 1960. That made me five years old, too young to be allowed into his room to visit. And however black the sky, it wasn't really midnight but the early dusk of winter, same thing to a child. My mom didn't drive in those days, so we'd caught a series of busses to get there. Hollow. Carved-out heart hollow.

"The World Bank," he said, "has a new staff physician."

I glanced over, studied his profile. Was it darker? "OK…"

"He told me I was in 'tip top' shape."

"That's good, right?"

"Yah, but…"

"But?"

"The new doctor changed my medications."

"That's weird, Dad. Why would he change your pills when they're keeping you in 'tip top' shape?"

"He says these are more effective."

"Do you *trust* this new doctor?"

His pause would prove historic, and if I could go back to that pause in the car with him, I would, even if it meant I had to relive all the years that have passed, even the shittiest ones. Finally, he said:

"He seemed like a good doctor."

A week later, in the mail, I received a letter from him penned on Hyatt Regency Waikiki stationary. In it, he said he would write again from Seoul. That very day, while it rained in a Virginia cemetery, we buried him.

Kiss-Kiss-Kissuni

Some memories lie dormant for decades, then suddenly spring awake, fresh as yesterday. I like to think the writer in me brought Kissuni back to life, but it was something else.

To me, a mere girl of seven, my grandparents' maid was a big-boned, strapping woman, always barefoot, always moving. Her feet were cracked clay; her face a rock. With mandatory bows, she led a back-breaking life of cooking, cleaning, ironing, and, like it or not, looking after me that summer. If I was thirsty, she brought me cool barley tea. If I needed to use the toilet, she carried me piggyback up a steep path that led to a church. If I couldn't find her, she was scrubbing dirty clothes in the river, chasing lepers from the front gate, or taking a meal in the closet where she slept.

No wonder Kissuni never smiled.

This was 1962 monsoon season in the mountainous fly-infested outskirts of post-war Seoul, halfway around the globe from our sweet brick rambler and blue morning glories in Springfield, Virginia. My world was a beautiful place. But here? Ugly. Forget drinkable water or indoor plumbing, even at my grandparents' house. And they were the lucky ones; the other villagers lived in mud huts no match for the treacherous rains. Here one day, gone the next—I saw it with my own eyes.

"This is where you come from, Fran," my dad, a World Bank economist who had fled war-torn South Korea eight years earlier with my mom, told me.

How could that be? My mom always brought me home clothes with Sears & Roebuck tags; here, the whole country was in rags.

My family had arrived in Seoul in style via first-class cabins in sleek jets and a luxury cruise liner across the Pacific only to be met at the airport by beggar boys with bloodied, bandaged hands wanting *American dollar!* Their desperation scared me—the minute we landed, I wanted to board the next plane home. But I didn't dare say a word to my parents, not one negative peep. I learned my lesson the time my dad and I drove past a rickety row of white shacks on the wrong side of Springfield, and I innocently quipped out the window:

"Those are poor people houses, right, Dad?"

He frowned. Deeply. "Don't call them poor people, Fran. That's not nice."

My dad, from whom I'd inherit a disdain for royalty, grew up in Korea under Japanese Imperialism. And these American shacks were castles compared to his childhood home.

With engagements in Seoul, my parents often left me to spend my days following Kissuni the maid around from room to room while chattering away in English—all pure gibberish to her Korean ear.

"Kissuni, let's go for a walk."

"Kissuni, it's a very nice day."

To my American ear, her name was lyrical—*Kiss-Kiss-Kissuni*—and I liked saying it, singing it, even if she ignored me like a fly she'd shoo back to America if she could. Why was Kissuni so moody? After all, *she* wasn't yanked from a summer of drinking Kool-Aid and riding her bike with friends. One time, for no good reason, she got irritated and closed, no, *slammed* the kitchen shutters on me so I couldn't watch her preparing lunch. Boo. Without television, the view of her spooning out rice, soup, and an array of side dishes was a main source of entertainment for me.

The day came when Kissuni cracked a smile, proving she was more than a stony stare.

"Beddy nice," she said out of nowhere.

"You mean 'very nice'?" I asked.

Her nod was like a deep bow. "Beddy nice."

Kissuni's *beddy nice* broke the ice. Soon we were inseparable, with our own language. *Beddy good. Beddy funny.* Memory: I'm on her back, we're going up a mountain, up, up, up to the church, me happily latched and facing her sunbaked, sweat-soaked neck. Life, every step, was hard for her. No string of pretty pearls in her future, only beads of perspiration.

"Biggyback," she said.

Some words might stump Kissuni, like the meaning of *fun*. Given her nonstop toiling, it seemed unlikely that fun, in English or Korean, was part of her vocabulary. Meanwhile, I was missing it badly: the summer carnival and Fourth of July fireworks at Springfield Plaza, the rusty swing-set in our backyard where one of the poles lifted out of the ground every time I swung too high. I liked Kissuni a lot, but I wanted to go home, and if left alone, found myself sighing, lost in daydreams. But the moment steam from Korean soup drifted my way—radishes and scallions swimming in fragrant broth—I'd float back to reality: Kissuni and me.

After serving me a bowl at the table:

"*Mas-issneum?*" she asked.

I nodded, wishing she could sit and join me. "Very delicious."

For someone who had to dine in a closet, she looked satisfied. "*Guk bap* beddy delicious."

Did she say—"Cook pop"?

Kissuni laughed. At last!

Every Sunday, she would leave early in the morning and return at nightfall by bus.

"Where does she go, Mom?"

Unlike my dad's English, my mom's was never perfect. "To family."

"But why doesn't she live with them?"

"They are poor farmer. No rice to feed her."

A child my age couldn't make sense of war, much less understand that Kissuni was a faceless casualty. But I did know that her portrait saddened me. Maybe it wasn't part of my glossary yet, but I'd learn to despise the word *hierarchy* the way I despised the closet where Kissuni ate and slept but didn't dream.

By summer's end, I was speaking schoolgirl Korean, and Kissuni was speaking schoolgirl English. Joined at the hip, we chatted from sunrise to sunset like we'd be chatting forever. But monsoon season was nearly over, and our time in Korea was up.

"We're leaving tomorrow, Kissuni."

Hushed: "Go home?"

I danced; I sang: "Yes, yes, *yes!*"

"Beddy good."

On the morning of our departure, Kissuni was permitted to accompany my grandparents to the airport. Queen-stoic, too proud to bend down to squirt-level, she held steadfast as I looked up at her. Sure, she was my buddy, but, honestly, I couldn't wait to land on American soil and do all the things I'd been missing, like dive into a two-scoop sherbet from High's Dairy, one orange, one raspberry. My favorites!

"Good-bye, Kissuni."

Try as she might, her emotional guard collapsed, and Kissuni wailed like an old woman in ruined rice fields.

By the time our airplane disappeared into the clouds, I forgot, no, not really forgot but rarely, if ever, thought about Kissuni again. I was too busy living my life. Growing up. One day I was a young girl, and the next day, it seemed, a young woman dreaming-writing-falling in love, over and over. So many chapters. Granted, at any point, if someone were to say, *Tell me about that long-ago maid in Korea*, I could probably do it, squint through ancient fog and drum up the image of a strong brown woman. Beyond that—hazy.

Decades after the summer of 1962, a more mature me was listening to my widowed mom reminisce about the good old days. Out of the blue, she mentioned Kissuni.

"She always want to learn."

I blinked, detached but trying not to be. "Yes . . ."

"So smart."

"Yes . . ."

"You teach her English."

"Right . . ."

In fact, how many English words did Kissuni memorize that summer? Dozens? A hundred?

Beddy nice. Beddy good.

"But she have no education," my mom regretted. "Too poor to go to school."

"Well," I nodded definitively, "she was a smart, good woman."

"*Woman?* She not woman yet."

"No?"

"No."

"Well, how old *was* she?"

"Fifteen."

So Kissuni, whose only pay was meals and a roof over her head, who carried me *biggyback* to the church toilet, was a mere child herself. *Fifteen.* No wonder she lost her temper a time or two. No wonder she cried like a baby.

Our Kissuni conversation was transporting. Resurrecting. Maybe her face had faded from my mind's eye, but her spirit flooded back to me, and I found myself thinking about her, telling friends about her, even naming characters in my books after her. It felt like the tiniest little whisper of an honor, if that makes any sense.

Kiss-Kiss-Kissuni. Last name unknown.

Now, every so often, I'll ask my mom what she recalls about Kissuni's fate, as if some lodged nugget might jiggle out of her brain, something old and gold and forgotten. But it's always the same story:

"She very sad after we left grandparents' house and quit."

Unlike mine, Kissuni's world was not a beautiful place. Indeed, it was ugly and unfair, and I will always wonder: She survived the Korean War, but did she survive her lot in life? I don't know. Did she marry a farmer, and, if so, was he a good man, and did he make a good living? I hope so. Is she even still alive? Only God, if there is a God, knows.

Death in Andover

All I know about the boy is that he was seventeen, a student at Phillips Academy and that he died at the train station. That he was of Asian descent made a gray day grayer. Atmospheric.

For me, New England is easy to romanticize. I was born outside Boston in Cambridge to parents who were part of a nearly invisible wave of well-groomed Korean grad students and their wives in the 1950s. You can tell from fading photos how well my dad fit in with the company of young foreign scholars who believed they would change the world. From generation to generation, we dream. Too soon, my family moved south to the Virginia suburbs of DC—my dad got a job at the World Bank—but Boston was always there, my hometown sitting in some mythical mist up north, and in the back of my head in my heart of hearts I believed that had we stayed I would've grown up happier with a real feeling of home, far from the madding hicks and mean girls. Granted, many of our neighbors were fine, and I loved the Lyle family next door, but telling people I was born in Cambridge, Massachusetts, was a source of pride for me as if I planted the ivy or was one with the ivy. Some ivy connection.

I'd been back to the Boston area before but never in October and never here, to Andover, a prep school town so picturesque in collective memories surely, it's always autumn. Staying at The Andover Inn, we'd flown in the day before for a post-wedding celebration—the daughter of my husband's good friends from college had recently wed in Tel Aviv, and now it was time for their stateside friends to get down and party in the Old Town Hall. American Jews, Israeli Jews, Colombian Jews—no one went out of their way to make me feel like the odd one out, but I wasn't one of them. Still, everything felt starry, in sky and spirit. People kicked off their dancing shoes and drank with abandon. Through it all, the bride was a vision. She wore a pearly thing in her hair.

The next morning, my husband went out for breakfast. For me, the echoes of last night's loud hip-hop-rock-salsa meant a quiet coffee in the room would do.

"Take your time," I told him.

From the second-floor windows of our sweet corner room, the town took on a gothic cast, looking more like a movie set than a place where real lives are lived. Peyton Place, if you're old enough to remember. I finished my coffee, then took a shower. When my husband returned:

"Well, I heard some sad news."

"Oh?"

"I noticed a crowd at the church next door, so I asked the person at the front desk what was going on. Apparently, a student at Phillips Academy took his own life last week."

My heart sank. No one wants to hear that.

"His memorial service is today."

Last night, a song; this morning, a hymn. I took to Google to confirm a hunch: an Asian surname.

Momentarily, the pregnant sky's impending birth dashed our plans to get a good look at the village shops and restaurants in daylight before heading out to Logan Airport. My mood had changed anyway. A boy was dead. This was his town. The view from here was so close to the streets and sidewalks I felt like I was twelve again, peering out the window of my parents' bedroom upstairs to see if the coast was clear. If not, I'd stay holed up in my room writing stories. Many lives were lived up there.

But back to Andover. My eyes were hooked as I spied on a stream of young mourners coming back from the memorial in packs of twos and threes, heads down. The occasional loner, hands in pockets. It was all very hushed. Black-clad figures against old stone buildings provided a timeless optic; it could have been now or circa World War II. Were these the boy's friends? Or just classmates? Did they attend the memorial out of respect or because the masters insisted? Did anyone know his despair? Did anyone care? To be fair, the procession was somber, but a little emotion would be nice. A funeral face or two, my God. Finally, a girl collapsed in tears before tearing away from her friends. I wanted to take a picture but didn't.

Then the rain came, hard and heavy.

Maybe you can relate, but I think more about death now than I did a decade ago. In the past year, I lost my soul-mama Tess, who was something, and a sweet dog Jefferson, who was everything. Sometimes when I think about getting old, the notion of checking out with a magic pill saves me. Not while I can still boogie in an Old Town Hall but when I'm frail and don't know night from day. True, it's tragic but not like a boy facing death head-on at a train station.

Generation after generation, we dream, then die. But at seventeen?

On the dance floor, the younger guests had hoisted the bride into the air. She was light as a feather. Champagne bubbles.

Meanwhile, a few blocks away, preparations were in place for a morning memorial.

One body up, one body down.

A soiree, a suicide.

A couple of weeks later, I'm still haunted. Why am I writing about a death in Andover? The boy wasn't my son. All we shared was the earth and an Asian heritage. Whatever went wrong is out of my sphere. When I mentioned I was writing this little reverie to my husband, he looked at me as if through ancient New England fog.

"Oh—did someone die?"

One day in 1979, my family buried my dad. Much like that Andover morning, it was October and gray, not a miracle in the sky. Let me tell you something: The sound of rain hitting the tarp over your father's coffin will break you.

The funeral was attended by hundreds, mostly Korean scholars from the early days and international types from the World Bank. Many years later, they're all a blur in the rain. Only Mr. and Mrs. Lyle remain standing, strong and loyal.

My dad's sudden death at fifty-six was natural, but he was still too young. His dream checklist, only half done. If anyone had the will to live, if only to take care of his family, it was him. He was our hero, our Hercules. But even he could crack.

A decade earlier—and here's where the story grows fuzzy because my memory is that my dad confided in me, but considering I was only about fourteen, maybe I just overheard it—I learned there was an incident on a plane during his World Bank travels. A feeling came over him, the urge to jump off. The feeling was so powerful that when the plane landed, instead of catching his connecting flight back to the United States, to us, he took a taxi to a hospital. There, he was sedated, having suffered what must have been a severe panic attack. At that age, I can't be sure how I coded it beyond a certain truth: my dad was more fragile than I thought. Maybe we all are.

Coffee with Catie

If I know Catie, she sipped her coffee for a spell before dropping a bombshell in her email: Catie, sweet Catie, is filing for divorce. Her burly husband, downstairs watching TV, has no idea. In a couple of weeks, she'll go on a "trip" during which time papers will be served, and a friend with a key (what friend with a key?) will collect her things, she explained before signing off. La-dee-da, but that's my Catie to a tee, half-sleepy, half-dreamy, coffee or no coffee; it doesn't mean her world isn't crashing or that she's OK; it's just how she is, crisis or no crisis. Calm. Catie's great escape, hatched in a dark-night-of-the-soul place without me, illuminates something more visible than tonight's blood-red moon: I wasn't there for her.

Once so close we nearly drew each other's breaths, Catie and I were always together, and if you were within a mile of our vicinity, you couldn't miss us because we cut a spectacular contrast: she, an angelic blonde wisp; me, a smoky-eyed Asianette. Maybe legends in my own mind. We shared classes, apartments, cigarettes, and beer, not to mention secrets, though not all, mind you, and coffee, endless hours sipping, cupping, blowing into coffee, leaving lipstick prints like kisses, all the while believing we could figure out our whole lives over a long coffee break, even though we never solved a damn thing last time or the time before. There she is, pouring half-and-half, now tapping the contents of a Sweet 'n' Low packet, fingernails Raven Red by Revlon, to create the perfect milky brew in Waffle House and Lendy's and Lum's; in two different student unions as we started out at one Virginia university then transferred to another, first me then she; even in a downtown DC office for three years with adjoining desks where, if we were too busy to run around the corner to Leo's Deli, we made do with weak-tea coffee from the Xerox room. Nasty stuff. At some point early on, Catie invested in a green plastic percolator that brewed coffee so strong my first cup had me laid out in bed like a junkie on speed, screaming my tits off. Meanwhile, she, a veteran coffee-drinker long before we met, casually puffed on her cig in the living room:

"It's just the caffeine, Francie."

In some abstract orbit, we're still living that life because once or twice a year I'll spot her on Connecticut Avenue or in DSW, not her but a heart-stopping version, a doll so small she might fall to her knees on a windy day, which the real Catie did on the Drillfield at Tech, and the thought of having coffee with my oldest friend seems like too much to ask for.

Tonight, ten o'clock star time. My husband and I wander outside to check out the blood-red moon that has the whole planet talking. Hug Bug and I are intelligent beings, but moon science is over our heads, and I tell you it's like the blind leading the blind. Living in an urbane 'burb with shops at our door, we find ourselves alone in a vast deserted parking lot shared by the likes of Kohl's, Dick's Sporting Goods, Starbucks. Look up, feel dwarfed. It's kinda cool, like being in a comic book.

"Where is everyone?" I wonder.

"It's a ghost town."

Hand in hand, we cross the hushed sidewalk toward Whole Foods, hoping for signs of life. One or both of us whisper:

"Civilization."

Several spectators are moon-gazing in front of the closed Whole Foods for a front-row seat. A man with a daughter points up, but why? Our moon-view is marred by an ink-blotted sky.

"The cloud covering comes and goes," the man says. "Just keep your eyes open."

I do, ready for the rare celestial event.

"Excuse me, do you know where we're supposed to go?"

Fall 1973, a universe ago. The first words Catie ever said to me were accompanied by her hand on my forearm. Her touch surprised me. College orientation was a zoo, and maybe we had exchanged a word or two earlier, but for all intents and purposes, we were strangers. In the same boat as me and the throngs of incoming freshmen being herded from room to room, she was lost.

"Not really," I said, glad for the chance not to be lost alone.

Chaos and confusion separated us, but within a couple of hours, our paths would cross again. There she is, in an empty hallway that was the English department, sitting on the floor outside the door of a college advisor with whom we'd both signed up for appointments. She sighed.

"He's a no-show."

Maybe I'm trying too hard to draw a parallel about the intersection of souls and stars and how fate aligned us, but was it dumb luck that we just happened to share majors and last names beginning with the same letter—"P"—and found ourselves merged in the same spot, waiting for an absent-minded professor who never showed up?

You know, I don't recall getting to know Catie. I only recall instantly knowing her. We had coffee. We talked. Unlike me, she saw only the good in people and didn't have a bitchy bone in her bod. Like me, she had a solitary bent, and I couldn't help but remark that approaching me at freshmen orientation seemed out of character for her.

"I know, Francie," she agreed, "I remember looking into the crowd and noticing only you."

"What did you notice?"

"That you were like me. Petite."

Actually, I towered over Catie, but she saw what she saw. Soon, we became each other's worlds.

A surprise Mother's Day lunch for our moms at Lum's turned out to be a dull affair of sandwiches and coffee and blank looks. Silly us, we were hoping our moms would hit it off.

Our dads, not a chance. Mine was a personable and engaging man who was concerned when he thought my new friend was ignoring him.

"Fran, why won't Catie *talk* to me?"

"She's not ignoring you." On the contrary, Catie was in awe that any father could be so nice. "Believe me."

"But when I try to make nice conversation with her, how come she doesn't answer?"

I witnessed this oddity with my own eyes: "Because she's not allowed to talk in the house when her father's home."

"What? What kind of man *is* he?"

Not the dad of her dreams. Beyond that, a mystery. Catie and I shared many things over coffee, yet when I think about it, I did most of the talking, and she did most of the listening. She could be private, nothing wrong with that.

FYI: Catie's father, having long left her mom, still wakes up and cycles around his neighborhood, enjoying retirement while mine's been in his grave so long he wouldn't recognize the earth today.

Not fair. Not fair.

But like a candle on a cold night, I'm warmed by a thought: Catie knew my dad. Saw him pass by my bedroom with a wave while we listened to Loggins and Messina. Outside of my family, to most everybody else in my modern life, my father is merely a mythical figure I talk and write about—a lot. Yet he was here once, and when I talk to Catie, he comes alive.

Indeed, the last time we spoke on the phone, she said she saw him in a dream.

We do stay in touch, but nothing's the same. On opposite coasts now, we may as well be on different globes, circling away from each other, still loners at heart. Distant, like it or not. Our husbands have never met, and I wouldn't know her cabin from another cabin in rural Washington state where cell phone service is spotty, and texts don't come in—which suits a girl who rarely checks her email just fine.

Sometimes I drum up an image of the room upstairs where Catie composes her occasional message to me, always long and thoughtful much like her letters of yore back when we spent those semesters apart, usually very early in the morning and so black outside the window she can't see the bears, if there are bears, in her backyard. There she is, profile lit by a desk lamp, drinking coffee from a large pot she nurses all day. And while she offers up reports about her health, her aging mom, the weather, no dark night-of-the-soul stuff to speak of. Well, a long, thoughtful email from someone nearly off the grid is only good for a soundbite here and there anyway, not the whole story. Like why she's leaving her husband—for sure, she has her reasons. Who the friend with a key is—not me, a million miles away.

But, too, I wonder: All the nights she's been contemplating divorce in a cabin in the middle of nowhere—what was I doing at any given moment? Drinking wine? On Facebook? Most likely not thinking about the one friend who was there for me the night I needed her.

Fellow earthlings gasp.

What am I missing? Even my husband, a guy who lectures about the Holocaust, has gone Gilligan.

"Look! See it?"

As a matter of fact, no. The cosmos is playing mean tricks on me, hiding the full picture: The blood-red super moon, they're calling it. All I see is inky sky. Rorschachs galore.

"There!"

There where, damn it? Meanwhile, everyone's clicking away paparazzi-style.

"Quick," Hug Bug says, "take a pic!"

Blindly, I *click-click-click* only to come up blank. I knew it. Waste of energy. Expectation.

"Let's go in," I say.

"Be patient."

So patiently I wait. And wait. And then, through a gauze of drifting clouds, a faint blood-red vision comes into view.

Cool, I guess, but . . . why do I feel like I'm missing something?

About this time of year, thirty-six years ago, a guy and I were making dinner in a shoebox of a kitchen in his green row-house in Foggy Bottom. The phone rang, and it was my brother-in-law Bob summoning me home. Home being the family residence out in the 'burbs.

"Everything is fine," he said.

I believed him because he was calm-sounding, not alarmed, though obviously handling a situation here—his wife, my older sister, was away on business, and my parents were in Hawaii, the first leg of a trip around the world they had planned and planned. In my mind, I figured my younger brother and sister, teens at the time, had squabbled. What else?

My friend drove me to the Arlington duplex I rented with Catie just outside the city so I could hop in my car and continue down the highway to the family home.

"I'll call you," I said.

When I went inside to get my car keys, I told Catie what was up. As if awoken from a dream, she grabbed her handbag and said she was coming with me. *Huh?*

"You don't have to, Catie."

"I want to."

"But—"

Insistent, she scrambled into the passenger's seat, and we drove down the highway listening to the radio because we always listened to the radio, unaware of the constellation above us.

Barely in the door, Bob directed me to the rec room and sent Catie upstairs. There she is, my Catie, running up the stairs. Who knows what room she went into or what she was thinking, but I do know she was up there the moment I learned my father was dead.

I read this morning that a total lunar eclipse happens only two or three times in a person's lifetime. Yet meeting Catie could only happen once. There she is, touching my arm, the timing magical as a meteor shower—I was no longer lost. Yet tonight I'm lost as ever, picturing her silhouette in a room three thousand miles away, wishing we could go for coffee.

Love in Yiddish

Whenever I've got the moody blues, I call Estelle. Maybe she won't remember our conversation tomorrow or the ruby-colored stone she slipped me when I was so low I took it for magic, but ever since the day we met to talk business in a long-gone eatery in downtown DC, she's been here for me, her whole soul pressed into the receiver:

"What's the matter, baby?"

That said, Estelle's no coddler. Ninety in June, she says whatever she wants to say, and sometimes I need that, a stern delivery issued with love.

"Goddamn it, quit kvetching. Life's a bitch, but you pick yourself up and dust yourself off!"

Heartache's her specialty. There's a reason.

We don't look like friends, and what a beautiful thing. Different generations, different backgrounds. But Asians and Jews often come together in the retail-wholesale world. In our case, I was interested in selling Blum's of San Francisco Chocolates in my shop, and Estelle was their local rep—thank you, Universe. God knows we've done our share of schmoozing at trade shows and candy counters, laughing our *tushes* off since 1983.

I miss those days. Miss her. Go for the phone whenever I grow nostalgic.

"*Estellgic*," says my husband.

Now she's retired, my very own Golden Girl in Silver Spring's Leisure World. If I find her in a prickly mood, I get it. More funerals than fun these days.

It's an art, I tell you, being Estelle. A dying art. Puffy blonde head, every hair in place thanks to a night bonnet she wears to bed. Still, five feet tall with balls makes her a commanding presence. I remember when I wanted to return an item to Bloomingdale's months past the policy date; she up and did it for me, welcoming a fight. Well, she worked at the flagship Woodward & Lothrop department store in its heyday—retail's in her blood. Sometimes, bless her heart, she still seems to think it's 1960 and Woodies display windows on F Street rule.

"I don't understand how young women can walk out of the house these days without a girdle to give them the proper silhouette. I *always* wear my girdle."

"Even to bed, Estelle?"

"Don't give me that s★★t!"

That's one of her golden oldies.

Such dialogue is a bit piercing to my husband. He's genteel—but not Gentile. Yeah, Jewish too, and while both define themselves by their Jewishness, the similarities end there. True, he once uttered the F-word in Walmart, but in his defense, he'd never set foot in a Walmart before, and that was his reaction. And this was Estelle's when I told her I was marrying into the tribe:

"Is he good in bed, baby?"

For a Jersey boy, my husband's an Old World Jew, bred on the Holocaust, the death camp stories of his Austrian-born father and the peasant soups of his Russian-born grandmother who gave him Russian lessons between ladles because sooner or later, the Communists would invade America, and if their precious boy could speak their tongue, the family would be spared.

Meanwhile, Estelle's an American Jew who'd rather talk about how she's hosting Passover for twenty.

"I'm all set. My brisket's par-cooked in the freezer, ready for the oven."

Not the torture, not the anti-Semitism. Too much already.

To both, however, stones have meaning. The one Estelle gave me, not ruby but precious, was a gesture of hope and healing. The ones my husband placed at my father's grave during his first visit, not flowers but symbolic, were found after a long, meditative search on the cemetery grounds.

Aside from the poetry of stones, the two don't really speak the same language. My husband's Yiddish is one for his fellow scholars, while Estelle loves tossing around juicy words from her Yiddish Word-A-Day calendars. Some days, everyone's a *schmuck*.

My husband calls me an honorary Jew because he claims he senses a Jewish spirit in me, and I don't know if that's true or just wishful thinking. True, I can make *matzoh brei* as good as the next old Jewish guy, and I can remember my first bagel a million years ago in the passenger seat of a car going over the Brooklyn Bridge—I'm digging my paws into a white deli bag, expecting sweet, not savory—and while I did write a humorous book about a Korean's boy search for a New York bagel and pen many an Asian American experience, I like to think more than anything I'm just me, Person. Though I won't deny my heart hurts more watching footage of the Korean War than World War II.

Jew, Schmew, you're just you, Estelle would say.

Thinking about it, maybe Estelle's girdle is her suit of armor. No jiggle, no wiggle—she's reined in and powerful. Brave. Glimpses of post-war life in America are like candy to me, and I've heard Estelle's stories, all of 'em. Soul-to-soul.

She survived Pittsburgh during the Depression. Her mother was pinched but loving; her father owned a struggling shoe shop. Three brothers, one died young, a beautiful sister, and a not-so-beautiful sister who married better so, see, you never know. The young Estelle took lessons at Gene Kelly's Dance Studio, even danced with him once.

"Wait—you danced with Gene Kelly?"

"Sure, Toots. Before he moved to New York and made it big on Broadway."

And then it happened: Estelle met a nice Jewish boy.

"Was he handsome?"

"A movie *staaaar*."

The couple married and moved to Baltimore, where life was

dreamy, and on summer nights, they'd set out lawn chairs and sit with neighbors, not knowing the honeymoon wouldn't last: Her young husband soon fell ill with Lou Gehrig's disease. The 1950s experimental treatment at Johns Hopkins Hospital proved futile—he died in Estelle's arms before their fifth anniversary.

For some reason, she rarely talks about him. Her references are stingy, even stoic, especially to someone like me who wants more gush, heat, pain, Estelle-coming-of-age, but she won't give. Can't let it out, feel lovesick over something she can't control. After all, she's Girdle Queen.

"He was a guinea pig, poor guy. What more can I say?"

Her Baltimore days behind her, Estelle relocated to Washington, and that's when her new life at Woodies began, first as a secretary to one of the merchandise managers before becoming a buyer for coats and suits. Along the way, she did what any young Jewish widow of her generation would do: remarry and raise children; in her case, on Flower Valley Drive in the Maryland 'burbs. I always got the feeling her second marriage was more for the sake of a desired if not expected Jewish lifestyle than love. And, after all that, a sad ending: At seventy-two, she was served with divorce papers.

Estelle was alone for a long time. Oh, there were her kids, a devoted bunch if there ever was one, and make no mistake, Estelle held court; extended family out the wazoo; synagogue friends and the girls from Woodies, but it wasn't the same. Maybe a bad marriage was better than no marriage, she'd lament. What she'd do to have a companion, at least.

"Someone to travel with and screw, goddamn it."

You can't edit Estelle.

Then she met Ed, a divorced, retired pharmacist with a sweet ambling nature. Even stooped, he towered a foot over her. In ways, it was a perfect romance—he let her be boss, and they did all the things they yearned to do with a loving partner: dine, dance, board planes and cruise ships. With his and her walking canes, no less. Ed wasn't some-

one who took anything for granted, least of all Estelle. The last time I
spoke with him, he was literally breathing with gratitude:

"I'm so lucky I found her."

After a few good years, Ed succumbed to leukemia.

Not long ago, we paid Estelle a visit. I adore her little museum
of a home, her personal history on the walls and tables: The Estelle
Archives.

My husband spotted a wall hanging covered in Hebrew holy text.
Wishing he had a magnifying glass, he explained this was a page from
an illuminated manuscript, produced in the Middle Ages by scribes
and artists on vellum paper.

"Fascinating."

Apparently, illuminated manuscripts don't appear on walls every
day.

To me, the star of the show was a black and white snapshot of a
young Estelle and her first husband playfully posing on either side of
a huge tree trunk. Peekaboo, I love you.

After blintzes and coffee, Estelle took my arm. "Follow me, Toots. I
wanna show you something."

Her decorated walls kept my husband busy while I followed her
down a little hallway, past the sewing room and a guest room to her
bedroom. Once there, she plopped on her bed like a girl clutching a
bouquet of flowers when, in fact, they were letters, tied-up in a bun-
dle. Love letters, obviously. From her first husband, of course.

"You never told me his name, Estelle."

"Sure, I did," she said as if she talks about him night and day. "Irvin."

Irvin. "Was he nice?"

"Oh, Gawd. A sweetheart of a man."

Just as my stone stays with me, so has Estelle's memory of Irvin.
Deep, tucked away, glittering. Damn it; she deserved that love. That
life.

"Do you ever read them?" I asked her. "The letters?"

"Sometimes."

Estelle's got kids and grandkids galore. But *bubbe* hugs aren't always enough.

"When?"

Screw the brave face.

Screw the damn girdle.

"When I'm blue," she cooed.

How We Rock 'n' Roll

The sky was moody the way moody writers like it, but historically, the Fourth of July was supposed to be a sunny rockin' day, good eats and bad ping pong washed down with Monkey Bay; Skip's fireworks show destined to join the others rewinding in my mind like a movie clip: I'm up on the deck, watching him, my bro-in-law, dart in and out of magnificent lawn lighting through the dazzles and the duds; he's in his thirties, his forties, his fifties, now sixties, half-Einstein, half-ZZ Top, the boy in him popping out year after year because, hey, the show must go on.

But the rain came and canceled everything. No memory-making for the reels today, folks, just me and Hug Bug stuck at home in a home that wasn't quite home yet because we'd just moved in, boxed in by the mad clutter of books unpacked and mirrors unhung, with nowhere to go. On the brighter side, the sunroom was set up, and since I can't live in Stars Hollow, this will be my little corner of the world. Got a desk, a bookcase, and a nook, a nostalgia nook, if you will, centered around my dad's Harvard chair, which I like to look at and picture him in. If that sounds eerie, so be it: His ghost is all I have.

Between us, Hug Bug is the bon vivant one, blessed to not know that kind of pain. Boned-in, deep as marrow. In 1980, a young thing, I had to call National Memorial Park to report that my father's grave was sinking, a reality that would prove symbolic of the days and years to come. Meanwhile, Hug Bug can pick up the phone anytime and call his dad in New Jersey.

Hug Bug twitched, looking outside. Fun was on the books—now what?

"Really? No Fourth of July at Ginger and Skip's?"

Ginger and Skip are their real names, and on more than one occasion, I've been mistakenly called Mary Ann. Such humor might be lost on Hug Bug. We're a decent duet, but sometimes I think we hit the high notes early. In fact, I suspect I hear the beginning of low notes. But the beat goes on.

"The rain might clear up," he says.

Oh, I doubt it. Highly. If I know my baby-faced sister, and I do, the all-day rain forecast was her doing. Don't get me wrong, Ginger's the proverbial hostess with the mostest, could win any throw-down you tossed her, even while gaining steps on her Fitbit and bouncing balls with her pups, but sometimes things get so crazy, it's like ten families and their pets live over there, leaving her a pile of ashes. That said, I suspect she woke up that morning with only enough steps in her to do a rain dance. She has powers, you know. Next up, a lottery dance.

Bookish types always have something to do, so we fall into our work—me in the sunroom, he in the living room a few steps away. Normally, silence is golden, but today, it's a dull chord. At some point, I put on a little James Taylor, mellow just the way Hug Bug likes it. Mellow's fine, but sometimes I have to draw the line.

"The first time I saw you," he expressed way back when, "I could hear Dusty Springfield singing "The Look of Love."

Like a lounge singer on *The Love Boat* began to croon with gushing emotion.

"Don't you *love* that song?"

Uh . . .

No. You'd assume Hug Bug's love of the Burt Bachrach songbook was a generational thing, but my God, we're the same age. Brought up in an old-world family, he remains old world and squeaky clean. But gimme rhythm and blues, baby—"Bell Bottom Blues" or "Let's Get It On"—something jazzy or sexy, something funky so I'll move like I'm twenty again, not elevator music for the wheelchair set. Well, consider our history: When I was working in a record shop, he was studying abroad; when I was cocktail waitressing, he was perfecting his Yiddish, probably by an oil lamp. Granted, no one ever said Jewish scholars who prefer footnotes over football are known for having rock 'n' roll in their souls.

Lunch at two, coffee at four. Half-asleep and off-key. Yawn.

Early on, when the enchantment between us was palpable, we would slow dance like the moon outside my condo was hanging in the sky for us and us alone. In some perfect little film, Hug Bug got up from bed one night, went down the hallway and into the kitchen, made clinking and clanging noises, then returned balancing two flutes of champagne and two little plates of chocolate cake. Voraciously inhaling it all, the bubbly, the sweet, the magic:

"This is what life is all about…"

How could I possibly fall asleep after that? Ever.

Before supper, Hug Bug hopped off the couch. I blinked like an old horse and wheezed:

"What's up?"

"Sax time."

A year ago, Hug Bug began taking saxophone lessons, and for someone who's the first to admit he's not a natural, he hooked up famously with his new brassy friend. Out of its case, the instrument cast a glow in the sunroom, and suddenly, ionically, a stage was born. My eyes lit up, a little.

"My teacher says I need to work on my musicality. Put away the sheet music and play from memory." With Shakespearean flair: "*Feel* the music."

Feel the music. Made sense. But what music? Lawrence Welk music?

"Let me serenade you," he said.

A serenade sounded promising. But Liberace-style?

After warming up, Hug Bug launched into a recognizable number: Nat King Cole's "Unforgettable."

Old-fashioned but smooth.

"Thumbs up, Hug Bug!"

A few pleasant rounds later, he suggested I accompany him.

"You mean *sing*?"

"Yes!"

"I don't know the words."

"Grab the sheet music."

"But I can't sing!"

"Yes, you can!"

As an adolescent, too young to drive and stuck at home, I fancied myself a songstress—the next Carole King!—and composed a summer's worth of songs that my mom, bless her heart, put to music. Our mom-daughter duet brought down the house, the house being a yellow colonial in the 'burbs. Seeing as we still laugh about them, our performances were legendary to us, at least, and I can replay them at will: She's on the piano giving it her all; I'm belting my fourteen-year-old heart out. But carry a tune today? Sing with abandon? Surely my voice was shaky as my soul.

Once, in my noncommittal days, Hug Bug said something to me on the phone that, for better or worse, was recorded for the ages: *Take a chance.*

I did back then. I took a chance. And now, in my ho-hum low-note mood, I thought, what the hell, take another. So, I sang.

"*Unforgettable* . . ."

Naturally, Hug Bug's reaction was buoyant. "You were great!"

Oh . . .

I was bad. Really bad. My ancient voice, rusty-wobbly-shot, embarrassing in front of anyone but Hug Bug, made worse sounds than my first car, a 1973 sky blue Pinto, would make if I tried to start it up today. But so what. It felt good to sing my guts out. Really good.

"Encore!"

Well, we missed out on good eats by Ginger, a sumptuous feast she'd whip up in the time it took to pour wine, and fireworks by Skip where, under stars and sparks, he'd slip in and out of view, an image I capture like fireflies, is he thirty, is he sixty, can't tell from up here on the deck. One less collective Fourth of July for the memory books, folks. Now autumn is around the corner, and I'm in the sunroom again, looking at a Harvard chair I'll be looking at for the rest of my life. A woman my age still missing her dad seems like a very sad thing, but at least me and Hug Bug ended the holiday on a high note.

Boobs and Bones

Behind the front desk, the staff, a youngish flock, flits about. In the waiting room, older women somberly scroll through cell phones. Well, we're not here to have fun, folks; we're about as thrilled as growing gray. Get in, get out, get on with our lives. I'm asked to sign in, which I do with a wobbly scrawl. Why can't I fucking write my name anymore? I hear a chirp:

"You can take a seat now. We'll call you in just a minute."

From my chair, the office dynamics become crystal clear, and naturally, Boss Bird, the one making a flap about a lost ladies' room key, calls my name. I say that as someone who's drawn to the sweet, quiet bird in the corner, not the loudmouth in the room.

"So, you have back-to-back appointments for a mammogram *and* a DEXA bone scan," she says.

Comic sigh: "Yeah, makes the day twice as nice."

Her smile comes off as superior. Well, it must be awesome not having to worry about old chick things. When I was her age out dancing all night, I didn't either. With a sparkly pink fingernail that could take out an eye, she points out shaded sections on several forms with strict instruction.

"Make sure you fill out here, here, and here."

Note: One of us is in a prickly mood.

Boss Bird scans the clipped paperwork, looking for something wrong. Ah, found it! "You didn't fill in all the gray areas."

Gray areas? You mean like the gray areas of mammograms and bone density scans and shit like that?

Twenty, thirty, forty minutes pass. Boss Bird would say I missed my window by not filling in gray areas, so I hang tight and not ruffle any feathers. Finally, I'm called back by a technician my age, give or take, with a wooden smile.

"Hello."

"Hi."

"We're actually going to perform your DEXA scan first."

"But I'm feeling a bit brittle," I joke, even though it's true.

Not a chatty one. Stony, but I get it; she's got work to do. Once I'm in my blue gown, she takes my height and weight.

"How tall am I now?" I ask, standing ridiculously erect.

She double-checks, squinting. "Five feet four."

"Hey, I didn't shrink!"

Blank nod.

Note: She's one serious Owl.

Owl leads me to a room where momentarily she's propping me in a variety of positions on the examination table with the help of hard-foam geometrically shaped pillows. The scanner moves slow-mo up and down the length of my legs, hips, spine. Are we having fun yet? I'm no baby but watching my mom advance into her late eighties makes me shudder at the cold, clinical snapshots of life such as this very moment. These stills. Been through my own hell, too; then-experimental fibroid embolization at Georgetown Hospital was successful, but when national news broke of contaminated needles planted by a temp rogue in the radiology department employed there that same week—oh, joy. The periodic HIV tests over the next year were a barrel of laughs.

Owl may not give a hoot, but I hear myself rambling to the ceiling anyway:

"You know, I had my first bone density scan around 2008, braced for the worse. I mean, I'd been told being slim and of Asian descent made me a candidate for osteoporosis like my mom. But the results were fantastic: My bones were baseline perfect; I had the skeleton of a thirty-year-old! Hallelujah, all those years of drinking soy milk and eating yogurt and taking Women's Day vitamins really paid off. But my next scan a few years later revealed a very different picture: Now I was Swiss cheese. Thank you, menopause."

Polite but disinterested: "Happens to many women."

As Owl inspects the film, I'm hoping she'll tell me something good, as the song goes. Tell me my bones are miraculously rock-solid again.

At the very least, tell me if I fall, I'll friggin' get up.

Wishful thinking—she's ready to move onto the next patient.

"I'll bring you back to the change room. Someone will come to get you for your mammogram."

Frankly, it's not like I ever flashed them at the Peter Frampton concert like I was dared to do, but I was happy to have them, my crowning glories. Thanks to the Pill, I was voluptuous, and everything I slipped on looked good on me. Yes, once upon a time, estrogen was my friend, but turns out it's friends with cancer, too, and I'm not sure I can trust it anymore. Yet I still need it, damn it, not for birth control or bigger boobs but for other private things. Speaking of estrogen-fueled issues, just last week, I took my sister to the hospital for a procedure five worrisome months in the making. In the end, thank the god of little sisters, she was fine.

The door opens. Fluttering in like a breath of fresh air is a new technician in a sweet butterfly smock. I don't catch her name; it's foreign, as is her voice. I'll call her Dove. She's thirty-five or forty, young to me, reading my chart. Incredulously:

"So, you've been through *menopause*?"

"Yes."

"But you look so young!"

OMG, all caps. I didn't even have to fish for that compliment.

"No, I mean it!" she says. "That's crazy!"

Note: I love her.

"Let's put this on," Dove says. Instead of wrapping me in the big heavy belt-like thing hanging on a hook, she opts for a smaller apparatus that snaps around my waist. She has life; she has spirit; her presence is nectar. I would like her anywhere, under any circumstances. "Does it fit?" she wonders. "You are comfortable?"

"Yes, yes, I am."

"Good. Ready now?"

Yes, I know the drill. I'm a big girl. Thrust yourself into a cold towering metal contraption that squeezes and squishes your breasts into pancakes from this angle and that angle, your arm here, your other arm there, hold your breath, don't move, you're an eagle, yes, perched to fly because you'll be out of here in a heartbeat.

Before I know it, Dove is slipping the apparatus from my waist. Instead of hanging it up, she works it like a piece of gym equipment. Open, close, open, close.

Snap!

"See?" she says playfully. "It's good for the arms, too."

Holy shit, *that's* what I was waiting for. A light, bright moment. That smile.

Between Us

In the early years—the 1960s—my parents would drive all the way to a little grocer below street level in DC's Chinatown, the only place to buy the makings for the likes of kimchi and mandu, dishes unheard of in a Virginia suburb with Mayberry airs. Tuna casserole, anyone? Meatloaf? Well, maybe my mom made those, too, but Betty Crocker recipes never made their way to my memory book. Meanwhile, a mere whiff of baechu—napa cabbage—and I'm right back in our sunny brick rambler, my parents just in the door.

Enlisting her daughters as helpers, my mom would show us the ropes, Sarge-style. Granted, sometimes she could be more military than maternal. As a girl, I had no idea she had been forced to leave her mother and a fabled life in the far reaches of northern Korea behind, had been captured by a Communist soldier, gun to her head. 1947, sixteen, alone. The eventual toll of war—three brothers dead, her mother's fate unknown—left its mark. No wonder her mood could be distant. No wonder she hadn't quite developed that lovin' mom feeling.

"Do like this, I say…"

Mother-daughter, her history between us.

If I was lucky, my kitchen contribution might be slicing little red radishes into thin coins for kimchi—a quick chore and I was out the door. Better yet, occasionally stirring the galbijjim-braised short rib stew. Easy-peasy. Aromatic! But a mandu meal meant my whole afternoon was shot: dip finger into egg wash, rim dumpling wrapper, drop small spoon of moist meat mixture into center, fold up into triangle, pinch closed. *Tada!* On floured wax paper, I'd assemble my mandu in perfect rows, waiting for a smile or nod that never came.

"OK, you go now, Frances…"

Tteok was a rare affair. Background: My parents were part of a trickle of Korean academics and their wives to this country in the 1950s, a good decade before the national quota system was revoked, resulting in a larger wave of Korean migration. That said, it wasn't until the late 1980s that rice cake shops popped up in our suburb showcasing tteok, sticky yummies encasing sweet red bean paste. And here I'd been calling them *duck* my whole life! Well, maybe my ears were American but not my taste buds—Twinkies, take a hike.

Tteok-making began with rice flour, beans and sugar, and ended with my mom dropping our hand-molded creations into boiling water before draining each one in a slotted spoon and lowering it into a large glass bowl with the others. Oh, almost forgot the finishing touch: a drizzle of sesame oil. North Korean legend had it that the prettier they turned out, the prettier your future daughters. My mom's tteok were like sculpted flowers while mine were bona fide blobs. That always got her chuckling. And then, with proud carriage:

"My daughter all beautiful."

To say she kept her family well-fed is an understatement—compared to my friends' suppers, our portions were sumo-sized. She could also whip up continental feasts for frequent dinner parties they held for my dad's World Bank colleagues and their wives, with an I-Dream-of-Jeannie blink. Later in life I'd learn my mom's secret, even if she wouldn't recognize the French expression: *mise en place*. The vision of our long buffet table lined with beef stroganoff, vegetable tempura, mini egg rolls, and my favorite Korean food—chap chae—warming in silver chafing dishes, was enough to keep me wide awake until the tea candles burned out, and all the guests were gone. To my disappointment, no leftovers.

After my dad died—his life robbed by an untimely stroke in 1979—my mom began to spend less time in the kitchen. No husband, children bigger now. At forty-nine, her role as the meal-maker came prematurely to an end.

"I'm mood for Victor's."

And off we'd go!

Pizza at Victor's. Chinese at Tau Tau. Tacos at Taco Bueno. These were the offerings of the day and, to my mom, it was all good. Over a four-decade span, our suburb went from Mayberry to multicultural, and our dining options expanded. My mom wanted to explore them all, forever carting home leftovers. I always lived close by and eating out was our thing.

"No more cook!"

During our outings, she would talk about her idyllic childhood, humming Korean songs on the way home. It all felt healing, and in time I knew everything.

Yet even toward her last years, one constant remained: Sometimes I'd walk in the door of the house she shared with my sister's family and find my mom hovered over a large skillet, her chopsticks going crazy, her face in fragrant steam. Oh, I knew what she was up to: preparing me chap chae. Honestly, I wished she wouldn't. Chap chae was not her favorite dish by a longshot and, moreover, whenever she stood in one spot for long, the pain in her legs became unbearable, followed by searing night cramps. Her old recipe required washing a mound of vegetables—carrots, scallions, onions, mushrooms, bell peppers, zucchini—and sliced so sliver-thin they got lost in the glassy cellophane noodles. Too much trouble.

Although I admit, a beautiful sight.

"All for you, Frances."

Mother-daughter, our history between us.

Koomo Who?

Maybe Koomo, a strange little blond guy in an Edvard Munch tie, always had a death wish. Because lo and behold:

Day twelve post-surgery. He's been moved from a cluttered, germ-infested ICU wing in one hospital to a sparkling rehab facility in another. Lifted and propped up like an eighty-pound rag doll. Sadly, it's kind of fitting for the lovable, dreamless, riddled, chain-smoking Koomo who's perfectly fine being tossed and bossed around, so long as he can go home to a bottle. But at least my friend's alive. At least that. Though I do wonder: Is he really my friend? And: Does he even want to be alive?

Some questions you ask the Universe and get nothing back.

In sweeter times, we were closer. He was Dude; I was Dudette. We carpooled and worked at the shop together. When he missed a day, I missed him. When he went on vacation, it felt like eternity. Once, he brought me back a little replica of a magic lamp from Dubai. It was so gold, so perfect for an aging girl like me who still dreamed like a teen. Alas, his gift was no dream-maker, but in the end, its charms on my bookcase were enough. But today, before leaving home, I stuffed it in my handbag along with a clutch of get-well cards. Maybe a magic bag of tricks would bring Koomo back to life.

Yeah, right.

The elevator opens to the fifth floor. *Finally.* Is it possible the whole staff can tell I have no sense of direction, that I'd parked in the wrong faraway lot and got all turned around and frazzled? Because every face I pass asks:

Are you lost?

Are you lost?

Are you lost?

All I know is this: If I'm in a dream, it's not a good one.

I step into his corner room, wishing we were anywhere but here.

"How are you, Koomo?"

He tears up, reaches for a hug.

Stage four oropharyngeal cancer isn't a pretty thing, and after six-teen hours under the knife, Koomo's not a pretty sight—I'll spare you the post-op horror show. Lots of gore still going on, but what stands out is his Franken-neck—two rows of monster staples above a huge patch of oozing, grafted skin. Like I said, not pretty. Barely able to crack open his mouth, he's on a feeding tube for at least six months. On the flip side, he can't smoke and drink. For now.

On his birthday last March, he wore the green Hawaiian shirt I gave him—buttoned it over his shirt and tie, silly guy—looking ready to hang out under palm trees and blue skies. Four months later, he's here, a drooling, matted-hair mess with open arteries. I'm broken-hearted, naturally. But mad as hell, too. How many times did I warn him this would happen if he didn't give up his goddamned Koomo lifestyle? He always smirked back like he was cool with that. Dying.

"You look good," I lie.

I don't have the heart to tell him that most of his tongue is history and that he may never talk again. Hang onto your boogie board, my friend.

I like it much better here, he writes. *Nurses are nice.*

Koomo got lucky with a spacious room and a big picture window. Beyond the parking lots and main road, a pastoral view. With childish puppetry, he points out a gleaming bathroom and a chalkboard mark-ing his hourly schedule.

"Nice, Koomo."

Something out the window has stolen his attention.

"What are you looking at?"

Were he born mute, his gurgling attempt at speech would be val-iant. As is, it's just sorry. I look out with him, expecting to see a car accident or a carnival across the field. Nope. Like a kid with an Etch-a-Sketch, he erases his last message and scribbles:

See the deer over there?

Normally, Koomo wouldn't notice deer. But, then again, these are not normal times.

In public, Koomo's been the heartbeat of our sweet little shop he calls his happy place for fifteen years, a sober marionette putting on a lively show with this customer and that customer. Everything good happens there. In private, he's a stranger who blasts the Cure, hoards junk, and drinks himself comatose in a condo he calls The Treehouse. Nothing good happens there. When you loathe yourself, as he often expressed, you ward off good things—love, fruit, praise—like a vampire to the sun.

One Monday morning, he showed up at work with gashes on his forehead, the bridge of his nose, and a big one above his lip. His explanation was nonchalant, as if he was sporting a new mustache:

"I tripped over something and hit my face on the coffee table."

"Because you were dead drunk," was my response.

No dispute. Even if he wasn't drunk, he'd never speak or stand up for himself.

Honestly, what pulls Koomo's strings?

Once upon that sweeter time, he printed off a picture of us together and framed it not just in any ordinary frame but one embellished with the words *Best Friends*. Even then, it made no sense. Had I knocked on his door to thank him that night, he wouldn't answer. No guests in The Treehouse, ever.

Over and over, I've asked him: *What the hell happened to you? What traumatized you? Think, think! Express yourself, man! Why are you committing suicide?* Even when he had a voice, he'd mime back with a hapless shrug or the occasional and emphatic *I don't know!*

Period.

I never understood it. I was there for him; he had someone to open up to. Share his secrets, his troubles, whatever. Yet he was unreachable, untouchable. A thousand times, I put my hand out, but not once did he take it. His blank refusals were . . . breathtaking.

A doctor of Asian descent comes in and checks him this way, that way, asks a few questions. I assume he's the plastic surgeon because I'd

heard that the doctor who performed Koomo's reconstructive surgery—removed a rib and turned it into his jaw along with a lot of
other fun stuff—was some super-surgeon with an Asian name. The
guy looks at me like I'm crazy.

"I'm the rehab doctor."

When he leaves, Koomo rolls his eyes, reaches for his boogie board,
and scrawls:

A nothing doctor.

We yuk it up like we have a million times at work, and for a moment, he's popped back into character like a Koomo-in-the-box,
pulling double duty as the shop manager and my go-to guy when I
need to talk, really talk. We've had some deep moments behind that
counter. A great listener is gold. Koomo knows more about me than
anyone on earth, the holes in my heart, the sweet and the scandalous,
the lovers and would-bes, and never judges. He also knows I adore
our shop but dream of more, of writing great stuff for the world even
though I usually settle for an audience of one. Historically, it's been
Koomo. The great listener. Solid gold. But what about him?

Does Koomo dream?

Koomo's late father used to refer to his son as a scholar and a gentleman. Addictions aside, it's true. He breezed through William &
Mary, and no doubt he could quote an English Romantic in the
same breath as moody lyrics from the Cure. That nature makes him
thoughtful in ways, sensitive to the things that broke my life, most of
all the death of my father so long ago sometimes, I feel like no one
knows he was ever here. Even though Koomo and I aren't as close
anymore—he drifted a little away from me, but that's what Koomos
do—I could always count on one really heartfelt email every July 17.
Except this year, of course.

"My dad's birthday was last week," I say.

Koomo quivers; he quakes.

I admit: "I missed your birthday note."

I don't say it to make him feel bad; and he gets it. In his stitched and oozing state, he breaks down, cries from some place that hurts every minute, an extravagantly painful sight considering his Franken-esque appearance and knowing what lies in the days ahead: seven weeks of chemo and radiation.

Will he make it? Does he even want to?

Once Koomo fell, so to say, it felt like the season of everything good—happiness, sweets, laughter—came abruptly to an end. Whenever we were behind the counter together, he'd gush on and on about how our shop was his life. Now that it's been two months, he's ghosted his happy place. Meanwhile, every day, a train of customers comes in to ask about him. The talk is Koomo-Koomo-Koomo.

But, really, Koomo who?

I fish out the get-well cards from customers that have piled up in the past week, and together we read each personal, handwritten message. Koomo's smile is faint, almost quizzical, like he's trying to remember a life already slipped away. Soon enough, he's distracted by something out the window. Ah.

The damn deer.

Spotting deer seems to be his high for the day. A nobler high than usual but in these shitty not sweet times, let's get down: What's in store for Koomo? Even if he survives, will he ever speak or eat again? True, he was always a quiet guy who'd opt for a pack of cigarettes over a sumptuous meal. But come on.

"Koomo," I begin, not divulging the fact that three-quarters of his tongue is gone, replaced with something called a tongue flap, "can I look in there?"

Obediently, he opens as wide as he can. Not very. In both a practical and metaphorical way, I wish I could pry his mouth open with a mini-jack and a miner's hat. Staring back at me is a dark cave with a little pink. I give up. I shouldn't say it but do:

"What if you can't eat again?"

He shrugs like a rag doll would, if it could.

"I'm guessing it wouldn't really bother you?"

He shakes his head.

"Koomo, I need to ask you something."

"Mm?"

"Can I write about you? *This?*"

For the first time today, he lights up. Grabbing his boogie board, Koomo jots down with record speed:

A guy with too many vices that he tried to keep secret. But had a heart of gold. Gotta put in scholar and gentleman?

Proofing his notes, he corrects the word *had* to *has*. Yes, he *has* a heart of gold, not *had*.

Afterward, he's exhausted. For now, all seems said and done. Almost.

"I'm asking for a divorce after the holidays," I blurt. My crappy marriage isn't news to him.

He scribbles, *Why wait till after the holidays?*

On my way back to the elevator, a nurse asks me:

Are you lost?

All I know is this: Get me out of this bad dream.

Once home, I realize something: Ugh, I forgot to give Koomo the magic lamp. And if anyone needs a magic lamp right now, it's Koomo. Hope, however false. In a handbag filled with aging girl stuff, lotions, and lipsticks, I dig around for it, growing frantic as if maybe it was stolen or disappeared into thin air. But, no, thank God, it's here. I can feel it, buried like gold. Like Koomo's heart. For now, all I can do is hold onto my sweet gift from sweeter times, and a glint of hope.

To the Man I Wish I Married

One long-ago Valentine's Day, I looked up, and there you were, the kindest man I would ever know, standing in the doorway to my office holding a single red rose. What I'd do to look up and see someone like you, so nice and wonderful. A young professor with soulful brown eyes behind dark glasses. Though we'd barely said a word past *Hello* in the hallway, I could read your face like a line from Wordsworth. Granted, I'm milking the memory, but indulge me; my heart's a bit destitute these days, and there's no poetry in that. Back to the story. Little did you know that I, fresh out of college and working at GWU so I could take free writing classes but mostly trying to figure how to get rich writing poems, had you on my mind as well. Daydreaming, fantasizing, take your pick. Scenario: I'm babysitting your two children while you're teaching a night class; when you come home, they're asleep upstairs—and, well, you can guess the rest. I never told you that, God no, you might think you had the upper hand, and we couldn't have that, could we? In my world, that royal status was mine, all mine; that's what I was used to, and I liked it that way.

Maybe you vaguely remember my boss, a mature Norwegian woman who ran the office for many years. Her wrinkle-lipped disdain for grad students and professors alike entertained me all day. Whenever I'd come back from coffee or a lunch date with a student, she'd scoff, *You get all da vinners.* Yet, for some reason, she thought highly of you, the youngest prof in the program. Was vocal about it, like a song she wanted me to hear—so, yeah, I had the low-down: You were twenty-nine, divorced, had custody of a little boy and girl, a good father. Hmm. . . the idea of you aroused me. How grown up, to date an older man. A *divorced* man. With *kids.* What a novelty! An experience, to say the least, and new experiences turned me on. Drinking, dancing, no strings attached. Hey, I was a young, free-spirited woman.

Whether a gift or a curse, I remember old loves like yesterday, and I remember you. Not just our first date at a crowded Clyde's when we were accidentally separated and seated at tables in different rooms, wondering if the other had a change of heart and split, and not just your grateful lust night after night, but your earlier life in Pittsburgh and other Pennsylvania towns, which you would describe as I sipped wine on your lap and you sipped Scotch and puffed on weed: How your father was a milkman who had an affair while your suffering mother stayed silent, how he gambled and lost the family house when you were away at your first semester at college and when you came back for winter break, what a surprise, no home and you had to figure out a way to pay the tuition; how your college girlfriend got pregnant and you married her, but in time, she lost that loving feeling and took off; how there was another girl after the wife and before me, a college friend named Janet or Janice who visited you on weekends in your green, doll-sized Foggy Bottom rowhouse, but when you told her to go away you felt bad because you never had that loving feeling. I've always enjoyed listening to people's stories, their history, not the boring bio but the bone-deep stuff, what made them, what broke them, and I, like a kitten on your lap, could listen to you all night, secure in my perch because the way your voice dove deep and real whenever you called me *Franny Bear* said it all. But.

Like your father, I wasn't faithful. Like your mother, you remained mum. I have no excuse except that's who I was in that old universe, someone who didn't trust love. You are who you are at different times in your life. Then, I was afraid to give you my whole heart.

Still, we had memorable times. We drove around the city in your "Tank" and wandered into open houses in upper Northwest where the bluebloods lived; hopped into your Triumph and ended up in Atlantic City where, in a movie-worthy moment, a squat woman with pancake makeup yelled at me for playing her slot machine. We dined and toasted wine glasses at Dominique's to celebrate the sale of your first book. We scouted out potential sites for the chocolate shop I dreamed about opening after my father's sudden death left me in need of a sweeter life. We shopped at your Safeway in the Watergate to cook in your cozy kitchen—you half-singing, half-dancing, always happy for my company—then sat down to dinner with your dream children who never fussed whether at home or at a dim-sum dive in Chinatown, not even your three-year-old son who always preferred mac 'n' cheese. Your daughter was older with a serious nature, but I got a giggle out of her when I styled her hair with my hot rollers. When the two went to bed, you often expressed your desire for more children—with me. My response was always mum. Then.

Over a phone call, you broke things off. *I don't want to see you anymore*, you blurted. Click. I sat in my office, quelling emotion. Whatever led to your boiling point is a mystery, but I guess you heard or saw something or just thought too hard about me and my obvious lack of commitment. My God, I never once called you my boyfriend. Not too long after, on a sunny Sunday morning, when I was in the Safeway near my apartment in Arlington, I saw you in line holding a basket of my favorite fruits. Without a word, I took you home with me. The breakup was erased, as though it had been a dream.

A year or so later, you told me you'd been mulling and decided to move back to Pittsburgh. Taking care of the kids was too much for a single parent with a full-time job, especially since finding a parking space on your block had gone from headache to nightmare, and your mom was more than willing to help you back home—but the truth was, you were resigned to the fact that a future with me was hopeless. I supported your decision. Maybe you wanted or expected me to fall to pieces and ask you to stay, but that would mean a future that included becoming a wife and stepmom. It's not that you didn't mean a lot to me. But I fancied a grander life ahead that included experiences on every corner of the earth. Still.

Our last night together, me curled on your lap, was a tearful one. The next morning, you were gone. That was that, I figured. Goodbye, forever.

But your letters began arriving in the mail, pages of long gushing love. You came back for a visit, and then another, always reluctant to leave. When you talked about moving back, my reaction was half-hearted. By the time you called me one afternoon in a breathless voice and said *I never came out and asked you so I'm asking you now: Will you marry me?* I was already gone, the sound of your voice like an echo from some ancient cave. I'm afraid I scoffed. Your proposal was absurd; I'd always known you'd marry me in a heartbeat.

My answer was no.

We spoke once, perhaps twice, after that, only long enough for you to learn that I had left GWU and had finally found the perfect spot for my shop in town.

As it turned out, my shop took up all my time, and the jet-setting life never materialized. Time passed, then more, and whenever love disappointed, I thought of you. How you showed up at my office and stood in the doorway holding a single red rose. How you gave me small stud earrings, the first diamonds I ever owned, for my birthday. How I cried in your arms after losing my father, night after night.

Long after you moved back to Pittsburgh—I was still single—your daughter showed up at my shop. I didn't recognize this beautiful, grown-up lady—ten years old the last time I saw her. She'd gotten a job in DC, and you'd encouraged her to come to see me. We made a lunch date and, while I held my breath, she filled me in on you. Happily remarried now, still teaching. A wave of joy, tinged with regret, came over me.

Not long after, you sent me an email. Your tone was polite but formal, as if we were strangers. I guess it had been a long time. When I tried to apologize for my old, cold, thoughtless ways, you seemed to have no memory of our true story, only that I was a great girl who loved to write. Well, it was ancient history. We went back and forth a few times, and then I let it go.

Eventually, I did get married. Alas, we were wrong for each other, and that story is over. But.

In a way, no story ever ends. If I think of you, the story continues. Granted, a kooky concept, but humor me, a woman neither young nor free-spirited anymore, going through a divorce and probably meditating too deeply for my own good. Woe is me, right? Hey, I'm fine. And even if I've romanticized you over the years, you were still a prince, the nicest man I ever knew, and what I'd do to see someone like you in the doorway, holding a single red rose for me today. That would be so grand.

That Lonely Spell

For one long semester in 1974, my heart was a tomb. I didn't know a soul on the campus of George Mason University—then, strictly a commuter college—and despite five thousand students milling around me, I felt like the only person on earth. However brilliant that Virginia autumn, everything, like winter before its time, was gray.

Off campus, the scene improved with dinner-and-disco nights with guy friends, no one heart-capturing, and life with my family at home. According to me, and surely the US Census Bureau, we were the only Korean family in West Springfield. My dad in the garage-converted den, my mom slicing red radishes in the kitchen, my younger brother and sister running up and down the stairs. In my sweet memory box, they're still there, in the yellow colonial with green shutters. Their shadows, their echoes. My family. Had I known my dad would pass away in five years—in one blink, gone forever—any focus on me would've flown out the window, but I didn't know, and so, whenever class called, I got in my sky-blue Pinto and inched closer to campus while "Ramblin' Man" came over the radio and mental rigor mortis set in: I'm alone. My walk in the wide-open space from the parking lot to the building grounds took a century. Driving, walking, nobody cares. I'm in a sea of strangers.

Flashback to the year before: I was happy. Well, I could always count on Catie for that; living proof that you can meet someone and suddenly your world, like leaves, turns colorful because somebody knows you. *Knows* you. We latched onto each other, standing in line at freshman orientation, signing up for some of the same courses that day. In a heartbeat, we were one, inhabiting our own private isle, if you will, sitting in side-by-side desks and on outdoor benches, hanging out between classes in a cafeteria curiously called The Ordinary where, after a dull lecture, a coffee with a cigarette or two accompanied by our own brand of humor, laughing so hard our faces hurt, was the highlight of the day. For example, at lunchtime, The Ordinary offered, among other things, delicious hoagies-by-the-inch, at a dime an inch (!). Whenever I ordered a five-incher, the sweet Howdy Doody counter guy would slice it, wrap it up, label the price with a magic marker and say, *I gave you a free inch*. I'd run back to our table, laughing my butt off. Whenever I was with Catie, life was a comedy skit.

The next September, she transferred to a small private college. Catie didn't abandon me, it was always part of the plan, but once she was gone, the party was over, the campus as I knew it went up in smoke. The Ordinary—literally—ceased to exist. What kept me going was knowing that I was transferring, too, in January to Virginia Tech, where I promised myself to try harder to make friends and be happy. With no idea I'd lose my father before the decade was up, I did and was.

The lonely spell was history.

Or was it?

Strange but true that in the breadth of more years than I care to calculate, at any stage in life—while carrying on after the death of my dad who remains forever in the den wearing his burgundy sweater because it's always cold in there; watching over my still very-Korean mom, forty-nine when widowed, eighty-nine last month; witnessing my nephew grow up, once in my arms, now from afar; running a sweet little shop since 1984 with all the customers and conversations, even adventures, that come with it; writing stories in silent rooms as I age and wonder when I'll put down the pen; experiencing my fair share of love and loss with men and friends and precious dogs along the way; and of course keeping in touch with Catie—hearing "Ramblin' Man" over the airwaves always brought back the ghostly chill of one long-ago semester.

This spring, the lonely spell returned, most notably in Wegmans on weekends when everyone's at Wegmans, and you're forced to park in practically another time zone. The lot and the sky, so massive you're reduced to a speck, a ghost, nobody. Don't recognize a soul in the parking-lot universe, only the eternity of this walk, which feels eerily familiar. Once in Wegmans, among a sea of strangers, it hits me: I'm stone-cold alone.

I'm also going through a divorce. Though relieved, I can't help but question myself, doubt myself, my will and power to move on, make a good life, a better life. The emotional shift from *we* to *me* is a solitary affair. That said, I often wish that Catie—who lives on the opposite coast and last week wrote in my birthday card, *Am so glad we met that day standing in line at GMU!*—would move back here. Then this feeling would vanish in a snap. Just like that. Over coffee without cigarettes, we'd laugh again so hard our faces hurt. But since that's more reverie than reality, I remind myself that we all have our stories, and we all have our lonely spells. If we're lucky, they'll be gone by next season.

Finding West Virginia

I like to think I did good by my forever-widowed mom, born into northern Korean pageantry only to end up in the Betty Crocker 'burbs of Boston then DC, but in one way, I failed her: I never got her back to West Virginia.

Not to that mythical place, anyway.

Name unknown.

For the record, it was a real place. In the summer of 1964, our family vacationed somewhere, I never knew where, in the hills of West Virginia—an odd choice even for my adventurous dad who was *not* born into pageantry yet wanted us to experience it all, big and small. But Koreans out in the sticks? In 1964? The proof is captured in two bygone pictures of our family looking decidedly hillbilly—blame it on the mountain air. I framed both for my mom, neither of which feature my dad, our trusty photographer, but, trust me, you can feel his presence behind each one. Breathing, loving, wishing now could last forever. This still.

He had fifteen years left.

Though I was nine, my remembrances are fuzzy things, at best; dandelion puffs in a breeze: our log cabin with other cabins situated around a semi-circle path where the sight of a big, squished lizard made me jump out of my shoes; a roped-off body of water I took for a river but more likely the shallow end of a lake where my little brother Sammy snuck onto shoreline rocks only to lose his balance and—*splash!* Afterward, my dad, who jumped in after him and saved the day, had fun teasing his only son with a singsong, "*The other day, who fell in the water and was rescued by Daddy?*" Over time, the musing shortened to "*The other day.*" Then Sammy became Sam, and the joking got old.

Curious how a little spot in West Virginia would become fabled in my mom's mind, but there it was, maybe half-there, floating, like a dream or a heaven, some long lost paradise, once real, now imagined, staying on her mind like Wind Song Perfume, and if you don't know the commercial, lucky you, you're still young. Funny enough,

there was no denying her bumpkin bone or two—she favored country music and cowboy shows—but, come on, West Virginia, of all
places? Here was a World Bank wife who'd flown first-class to Paris,
Rome, and Hong Kong; dined sumptuously in Tokyo's Imperial Hotel, walked the shores of Maui back when the beaches were bare, and
devoured so many pastries while stuck in an Istanbul hotel room she
returned to the States downright pudgy. Still, the call of West Virginia
proved the loudest. Whenever I found her in the kitchen studying
the Travel or Weekend sections of the paper, I could predict her next
words:

"Where we were, I wonder?"

"I wish I knew, Mom."

"Listen, you hear story?"

Only a hundred times. The story: The only doctor available in those
parts happened to be Korean, and the locals worshipped the West Virginia ground he walked on. Apparently, when they saw us, they saw
him and welcomed us with open arms.

In 1964 America, the kindness of strangers wasn't something a Korean family took for granted.

On occasion, to perk her up, I'd get out our AAA Road Atlas, and
we were the blind leading the blind, tracing every inch of West Virginia with our fingertips. Though it was her nostalgic journey, I'd go
along for the ride. *Could it have been this town? What about that town?*

We may as well be looking for buried treasure.

"Why do you want to go back there, Mom?"

"Just do."

If only I knew where, I'd take her there in a heartbeat. Hitting the
road was our thing, and there were many little scenic trips, some even
to West Virginia—Shepherdstown, Harper's Ferry, Charlestown. Nice
jaunts, but no magic mountains to speak of.

Yet, one autumn Sunday, a sort-of boyfriend—meaning, he didn't
last long—and I took my mom on a day trip to Winchester, Virginia.
Nicknamed the Apple Capital, it was an hour and a half away and not

far from the West Virginia border. A historian who talked a lot about the Civil War, he stopped the car at one of the battleground sites where all I recall is a cannon on a cliff under ominous skies. Afterward, we ended up in the Old Town and walked around a picturesque village square, though for some reason, most of the shops and cafes were closed. Before returning home, we decided to drive farther out. All the while, my mom was poking her head out the window.

"Hey, where West Virginia?" she wondered aloud.

The would-be boyfriend explained we could practically toss an apple there. Pointing: "In that direction, Mrs. Park."

Even as we left the countryside, my mom kept glancing back at some elusive Eden. Not so much because the locals had been hospitable, but to recapture who she was as a young mother and wife, before widowhood.

Of course.

In years to come, she would bring up that day trip to Winchester, how she had the very certain feeling we were close to that enchanted spot of so long ago. Could smell it. I kept my doubts to myself. Winchester was too close to home, and if I knew my dad, he would've rented a log cabin deep into the Mountain State, or not at all.

Last August, the morning after my mom died, I went through some of her drawers, specifically the two in her coffee table. Just to touch her things. Feel her. I came across a hodgepodge of hearing aid batteries, old remotes, a half-dozen deck of cards—my mom did love her Solitaire, Korean-style—when something stopped my heart: a folded map, face down. I turned it over, dead sure what I would find: *West Virginia. Official Highway Map.* Most likely, she picked it up at a visitors center when we were on the road, slipped it into her bag without a word. The map was well-worn enough to tell me that her yearning was even more desperate than I realized.

Later, wondering how my mom could've read the fine print, I went through her drawers again. And there it was: a magnifying glass.

Time blurs, but that night or maybe the next or a week later, I got out my big box of collected family photographs, hundreds if not thousands of pictures, some dating back to before I was born. Every so often, I go through a few, have a memory or two, then put the box away. But that evening, I wanted to look through them all, even if it took me until morning.

Reaching in blindly, the first thing I pulled out was a small brown paper bag. I peeked in to see old-time slides, four of them. One by one, I held them to the light. The black film cast an eerie effect, and all I could make out were figures in fog posing like some ghost family. Wait, these were the same images framed in my mom's room—not a ghost family, *our* family. In the foreground of mountains, next to a log cabin. Our family, minus my dad, of course. Yet, in a way, he was there, always there. Proof: Written in blue cartridge ink on the bottom of each slide was his recognizable script: *W. Va Summer 1964* or *Bobcock State Park July 1964.*

The internet corrects my dad's spelling as *Babcock* State Park, located in Fayette, West Virginia, two hundred and fifty miles from Winchester. Not that the discovery mattered anymore. I put the box away.

In my dreams, she's still alive; we're moving through doors, through stores, making our rounds. When I wake up, the veil of reality comes over me.

As deaths go, my mom died peacefully at home. In a sense, she'd already left, no idea I was holding her hand. Speaking of hands, two days earlier, seemingly in a death coma, she did the unexpected: put her hands in prayer. For all our time together, in the end, I couldn't hear her prayer; I could only hope she found her West Virginia, after all.

Hey Judy

In the eighth grade, I met Judy. A twig figure with a brunette bob, she was the new girl who latched onto me as if I was her "in" to the popular junior high crowd. She saw me as the It-Girl. Who, me? The only Koreanette in late-sixties white suburbia? Well, I did wear long delinquent bangs and tease my hair, as girls did in the mod era, and sported kohl-rimmed eyes and silvery lipstick, when my parents weren't looking. Oh, and the flowery miniskirts, they did fit nicely. So right or wrong, maybe I liked Judy because her fawning gave me a crown of confidence I sorely needed. But I also enjoyed her company, listening to the Beatles and singing "Hey Jude" with so much angst you'd think we wrote the song and knew Jude so well we'd lay down and die for him.

"Hey, Ju-u-u-u-de . . ."

Man, we sang our hearts out.

Sooner or later, you knew Judy was messed-up; you could smell it on her like the Ambush cologne she shoplifted from Drug Fair. Her self-worth was a trinket, less than the gobs of stolen earrings she fanned out to certain girls in the hallway like Lifesavers.

"Do you think Debbie likes me?"

"Did JoAnn smile at me?"

How pathetic. "Judy, why do you care so much?"

"Because they're popular. And pretty."

They had nothing on her except future pompom status—consumed with an ugly duckling complex, Judy had no idea she was the true beauty. Or had the makings. At thirteen, she was too bony with a dorky 'do and needed a few Twinkies and time to bloom—no one in eighth grade paid her any attention, no matter how hard she begged for it. Despite Judy's troubling behavior, I was never alarmed. Someday she'd straighten up. For now, we were juveniles, and she was just doing juvenile things in-between soulful rounds of—

"Hey, Ju-u-u-u-de . . ."

Her family lived in the boonies, and Judy was embarrassed for anyone to know that she had to sit on a bus for an hour to get to school. Since hanging out wasn't always an option, we ended up talking a lot on the phone at night. An only child with a stepmother back when most girls had their real moms, Judy was always hiding in a closet somewhere, her voice dropping to a whisper:

"My father hates me, Francie. My stepmother even more. They don't want me around. Sometimes . . . I even think they want me dead."

One Friday after school, I took the bus home with her to spend the night—there were only a handful of kids onboard. The country roads were long and bumpy. Judy groaned.

"Welcome to the middle of nowhere."

From the outside, her home was something of an estate, but inside, a house of horrors. The Hitchcockian airs were real, emanating from her stepmother, a shrew who did nothing but sit at the kitchen table and smoke. I can still hear her cruel, nasal voice, which only now occurs to me was a low-class New York accent.

"Judy, why do you do everything in your power to look ugly? Why can't you be more like Francie?"

"My Gawd, Judy, you're lucky Francie will even hang out with the likes of you."

Later, in her bedroom, Judy wailed, "I can't wait to get *out of here*! I just want to run away and follow my dreams."

"What are they?" I wondered. My dream was to move to Hawaii and write poetry with leis around my neck. Period.

"Oh, I dunno," she replied. "To be a Beatles groupie."

"What's a groupie?"

She grinned and put on the White Album.

The next morning, in my only vivid memory of the man, her father drove me home. Like Judy, he was darkly attractive, a movie star compared to his wife—they made a strange couple, and I always thought there was a story there right out of *The Twilight Zone*: A hag wife with the heart of a monster, a handsome husband with a heart of stone. Anyway, Judy came along for the ride while her father drove in silence, seemingly poisoned with resentment at her, at me, at the world. Seriously, the son-of-a-bitch didn't breathe a word, not even when I got out of the car with a polite thank-you. When they took off, I felt sick to my stomach for my friend.

Blame it on the kohl eyeshadow, but I had the look of a girl more experienced than I was, which wasn't saying much, seeing that I'd never even been on a date. That said, there was a big, awful brute who used to pass me in the hallway trying to mutter obscenities in my ear like, *hey sexy*. I should've reported him, but this was 1969—the thought never entered my mind, only ways to avoid him. Meanwhile, Judy was titillated as if his mutters were sweet nothings.

"Did you hear what he said?"

"Who cares? I hate him."

"Why? He thinks you're sexy!"

On my way to gym class one afternoon, the brute grabbed my arm and pinned me against a row of lockers—I remember a classmate running down the hallway, screaming. The next thing I knew, he was mauling me and planting kisses all over my face and neck until I somehow broke loose. When I told Judy, and only Judy, what had happened, she cried with jealousy.

"You're so popular!"

For Judy, it wasn't *all* about popularity. We had plenty of good clean fun at my house, baking cookies and playing cards. The only photograph I seem to have of me at age fourteen, Judy took. It's April—my birthday!—a warm sunny afternoon in the backyard. I'm wearing a buttercup-sleeved pale yellow sweater posing with a fake flower to my face. I took a similar Polaroid of her, which she kept. Later, we played ping-pong in the basement. She never wanted to go home.

But that summer, while on a road trip with her parents, Judy derailed. In her only letter, she wrote, *You've seen one mountain, you've seen them all. I can't live like this anymore.* As September and the start of high school drew near, I got a series of disturbing phone calls from her. One call was about how she was taking all kinds of psychedelic drugs and had lost her virginity to an older boy who lived a few doors down. *Francie, we fucked and fucked and fucked!*—her lingo, not mine. Needless to say, I was speechless. Another call was to let me know she had run away from home and was living in an apartment with a bunch of hippies, all of whom she was, quote, fucking. Her tone told me who was wearing the crown now.

"If my parents call you," she instructed me, "don't tell them where I am."

They never did.

By Labor Day, the phone went silent and Judy fell out of my life. I always assumed she got busted in that apartment and was placed in some rehabilitation facility indefinitely, as I have no memory of her in my high school hallways. But who knows.

All I know is that I did see Judy again, twice.

The first time was in the early 1970s at a Badfinger concert. Badfinger was the first band the Beatles signed up on Apple Records, and *No Dice* was one of my favorite albums of the day. In the front row, I spotted Judy on stage with the band, sitting on a chair to the side and looking every bit the part of a gorgeous groupie.

The last time I saw her was around 1980. By then, I was in my mid-twenties and working not as a poet on an island but in a down-town office, coming home on a crowded standing-room-only sub-way train, jostled this way and that. Through a web of people, I caught a woman staring at me. The weird thing is that her eyes were dead, the eyes of a mental patient or heroin addict. Was it . . . ? No, this woman looked forty-five, not twenty-five, no trace of youth or beauty but . . . yes, somehow the stare told me it was Judy. Don't ask me why but we, who once sang "Hey Jude" with more blues than the Beatles ever intended, didn't exchange a word.

So . . . the story was supposed to end there, but after writing this ode to a long-ago friend who deserved better, curiosity got the best of me, and I made the mistake of looking her up online. Unearthing can be dangerous, and while I knew Judy's was no sweet coming-of-age story, any hopes that maybe, just maybe, she cleaned up her act and found her way, were buried. Judy, who really just wanted to be loved, is currently in prison for life. Her criminal record is unspeakable and sadder than any song.

Slow Dancing with Stan

Once my husband and I decided to divorce, I began slow dancing with Stan. Not with Stan the man—whoever he is today—but the golden boy next door back when my twelve-year-old heart was spinning like a top. Now slow down…slow down…slow down, girl, and just dance. The end of my five-year marriage was anticlimactic, less traumatic than breaking a crown. That's what happens when love waters down to weak tea. You end up with a non-love story and maybe a few cryptic notes. The good news? No heartbreak. The bad news? No heart to break.

I'm not saying I'm fine. Got a different kind of heart failure. If I close my eyes, maybe, just maybe, I'll come out of this coma and feel like my old self again and quit beating myself up over how I missed the signs and lost my heart to someone I didn't really know.

But screw all that. I'd rather be slow dancing with Stan.

If I could color in a little background, just to make it real for me again. Feel my heart. The neighborhood was new, four model homes and a mailbox at the corner entrance, green lawns, no trees. Our house was a yellow colonial with forest green shutters. His, a white-split level with black shutters. A bedroom window upstairs offered me a bird's-eye view of his backyard, specifically a patio that often served as a basketball court for Stan and his friends. The sound of thirteen-year-old boys laughing and shooting hoops had me—a bookish, bespectacled girl—flying there. Adjust glasses, zone in. He was taller and blonder than the others, with the look of a teen heartthrob and the moves and manners of a prince. Naturally, I wasn't the only girl in the neighborhood crushing on Stan; we all were. Did I have a chance? A chance for what? Really, I just wanted to dance.

Notes.

One late winter night, I was put off that my date had parked a good five blocks from our destination, a tapas bar. Freezing, but couldn't bitch. We were brand new together, and he was buoyant, a giddy shadow on the sidewalk as we walked in the lit-up city, swinging my hand like a schoolboy with his first girl. *I feel so happy*, he kept saying. Overkill, but I was charmed.

One early spring morning, as I was gathering my things to go home, he caught me off-guard by playfully pushing me onto his bed and falling on top of me. While he whispered sweet nothings—*I really meant what I said, I love you, would do anything for you*—I stared back and blinked, taking in his face. He didn't want me to go, but I had to go, which made me yearn for him when I drove away.

One late spring afternoon in Barnes & Noble, he took my arm for a dance in the aisle. Normally, I wouldn't put on a show, but he was leading, and it was obvious by his moves he favored Burt Bachrach over Stevie Wonder. I thought this guy I pet-named Hug Bug would always be this way, light, bright, and embarrassingly corny.

That we lived two hours apart didn't stand in our way because we were perfect together, cerebral types who put pen to paper, though my work was soulful, not scholarly. Both liberal, both vegetarian. He was sweet and soft-spoken, just the way I like it. He wrote love letters, which I devoured because words mean a lot to me. He begged me to take a chance, which I did because it felt molecular. Poetic, even. *We were made for each other,* he said a thousand times. *You're the love of my life!* I loved it, began to broadcast it.

My friend Esther looked concerned over sushi at Nooshi, our favorite downtown spot. She knows everything in my love life, as it happens. "So soon? You two just met a couple of months ago."

Stop. Take a break. Slow dance with Stan.

Stan's sister Robin and I were the same age, and I was often at their house. An upper-level sun-flooded kitchen off the deck set the tone for a happy, if not hushed, household, always a few degrees colder than mine in the summer, and for some reason, though my crush was four-season, it's always summer. Good vibes. Curiously, under their roof, Robin—not Stan—was my focus, as if the laws of physics said so, and I recall sitting with my friend at the piano, in total awe of her

fingers lightly plunking "Mrs. Brown, You've Got a Lovely Daughter."
Stan remained in the background, more her brother than the boy who
made my heart do back-flips at the window. When he did come into
view, he was unfailingly polite, always greeting me like an equal, not
some punk. *Hi, Frances! How are you today?* Then my clouds would
clear, and I'd see him for who he was, and my eyes would dance and
dance and...

Notes.

Six months after we met, we got engaged and bought a decorative
pink memory box at Home Goods to fill with mementos of our love.
Pity the poor souls wandering around Costco and Whole Foods with
lesser loves and no poetry and, hence, no pink memory boxes. Our
weekends were delicious, every minute of every hour. We slept lip to
lip and didn't move all night.

"Let's see that ring," Esther said, taking my hand. Back at Nooshi,
catching up. "It's beautiful," she murmured. But did she hesitate?

Of course, she did.

Time to drum up the fantasy, a slo-mo whirl and twirl with the
boy next door.

Catch your breath—there he is, right outside the bedroom window.
The golden boy. His blond highness. Adjust glasses, zone in. All I feel
is the longing in my heart.

Notes.

As it turns out, Hug Bug and I were not made for each other. I'll
spare you the blog and draw you a sketch: for me, it had to do with his
emotions or lack of. His so-called love seemed more staged than real.
When I needed it, it just wasn't there. Among many turning points:
The night I got word my great friend Tess was dying, he did not, did
not, did not comfort me. He was a dead tree. Deja vu the night before
we put Jefferson, my family's dog, to sleep. Deadest tree in the forest.

We could talk politics, food, writing, just fine. Friends and family, too. But soul-to-soul? Dead trees don't talk.

Day by day, that couple walking in the night, face-to-face on the bed, dancing in a bookstore, disappeared like shadows into ghosts. *I love you* gave way to *Luv ya.* Texts with *xos* and heart emojis—sweet nothings for nuthin'. He still inscribed *You are the love of my life!* inside every special occasion card, and I'd wince inside. What fakery—his scribble, my smile—and there were no special occasions. Cards would sit on the mantle for a week before I'd toss them into the pink memory box, never to see the light of day again.

We became the poorest of souls.

More notes.

One winter afternoon, he was making the hundred-mile drive here. The weather report was calling for flurries, but I kept looking out my window, praying for a blizzard, not this dusting. Desperate to be alone, I called him and said the snow was coming down heavy now and he should turn around before the roads got worse. He did. Granted, I felt a little guilty for the rest of the snowless day—but my little white lie brought me as close to wedded bliss as I'd felt in years.

Curiously, one not-so-long-ago Sunday in Wegmans, we were shopping for the usual good bread, bananas, his German coffee, etc. As we approached the floral department, I was shocked to get a final glimpse of the old him—youthful, uber buoyant—rushing up to the florist with, *I want to buy flowers for my wife!*

The next time Esther and I met up for sushi at Nooshi, I relayed the Wegman's incident to her. I thought maybe she'd say something like, *Oh, he still loves you* or at least, *Aw, how thoughtful,* so I could feel better about the marriage, if only for tonight. Instead, she frowned.

"That's annoying."

Yeah, I suppose it was a bit over-the-top.

End of notes. A true yawn compared to the lush capture of slow dancing with Stan.

Watch us, world; we're moving in mist, in moonlight, on a heavenly plane where only twelve-year-old girls in buttercup yellow dresses go.

I'm in heaven here, safe in his arms where our romantic round and rounds never advance beyond a slow dance, not even to a kiss. Because it was always more the dream of Stan, than Stan. Something pure and innocent to believe in.

One post-note.

There *was* a sign. Last week, while rummaging around in my jewelry box, I came across a lone heart-shaped earring. This time, the symbolism wasn't lost on me.

In a charming little seaside gift shop in the late 1990s, I fell in love with a pair of mother-of-pearl earrings with silver hooks. I wore them every day, everywhere, for years. Not only were they heart-shaped, but they also had the swing and the sheen, the look I love. When I wore them, I felt like me.

A few weeks after meeting my husband, I noticed one was missing from my earlobe and freaked. After tearing my condo upside down with no luck, I called TJ Maxx, where earlier that day I'd been trying on clothes. They checked their lost-and-found box—no luck. What about the dressing rooms, I pressed them. They checked—no luck. Two weeks later, I called TJ Maxx again to see if my missing earring might have turned up in a broom or a snagged sweater. No luck.

To be fair, my husband did purchase a pair of silver heart-shaped earrings as a replacement. They were exquisite but not the same. When I wore them, I felt like someone else.

Enough. The marriage died. *Pfft.* The good news? No heartbreak. The bad news? No heart to break. Yet it's not about finding love again; it's about feeling alive again. So, give me a gorgeous reverie not-of-this-earth any old day. Who cares if it's too abstract to be true, let me cling to the memory until my heart, for whatever it's worth, circles back to me. Because someday this period of my life will fade like my love for a stranger. But slow dancing with Stan? Oh, man. *That* will last forever.

So, dance, girl, dance . . .

A Comic Spirit

In an airport in San Salvador, a caricaturist named Adolfo flipped the cap off his black marker and began. Fast strokes, furious squiggles, it was always a gamble, but such was the life of a starving artist. On paper, his unsuspecting subject, a businessman, appears content, buoyant even, puffing on a cigar back when the earth was a different place. No, no, I don't mean world politics or global warming or no-smoking-in-public policies, screw all that. My dad was alive! He was here, once. Breezy and charming. Look at him, an impish man-of-the-world, hands on hips as if, duties done, he'd flung his briefcase and jacket to the wind. Curiously, the portrait isn't dated, but the narrow tie, short sleeves, and continent all point to the summer of 1967—South America was his beat in those days. Peru, Ecuador, Paraguay, Uruguay, El Salvador…Thank you, Adolfo, for capturing his comic spirit in record time, for immortalizing him, for having the guts to ask a perfect stranger for money in exchange for a scrap of paper, even if you and I are the only ones who know it's gold.

"My Heart Will Always Be with You"

Say it was a night, any night in the early 1960s, and I was falling asleep in our brick rambler on Layton Drive in the sleepy DC suburbs. Corner lot, the two-trunked tree. A basement that, like every basement here, flooded after a hard rain. The collective moan meant everyone on Layton Drive was in the same boat, headed downstairs with our pails. Still, we, the Parks, were different from our neighbors; the only family that ate kimchi, for one thing. Kimchi with tuna boats, kimchi with spaghetti 'n' meatballs. I even liked it old and soggy, but soon enough, my mom would fit herself with those yellow Playtex gloves over an impressive mound of chopped cabbage and sliced red radishes topped with cayenne pepper. Translation: new kimchi! Fresh and crunchy, just the way I loved it.

By the time I came to understand why only we had kimchi on the kitchen table, I had begun to love it less. Once, when a friend caught sight of a kimchi jar in the refrigerator, I panicked and told her it was fruit salad. Well, that was a different universe.

And in that universe, whenever my dad came in to say goodnight, I'd stir awake, soaking up every whisper, his gushing heart on display. My mom was another story. If on a night, any night in the early 1960s, I'd woken up to the sight of her tucking me in, I would've assumed it was a ghost or a mirage, my eyes playing tricks on me. Because my mom was far from the queen of affection. And she wore it like a crown.

"I'm no lovey-dovey like daddy."

And yet she was lovable, a character for the ages; a bit Desi, a bit Lucy, Korean-style—her war-torn history had left her excitable with the cutest kooky bird English. Well, it couldn't have been easy to give up her native tongue during the Japanese Occupation only to end up here after the Korean War, stammering to get the words out. A dummy was a *dumb-nutty*; affordable housing was *h-h-h-horrible housing*. And while smothering her kids with hugs and kisses was out of the question, how could we not love our unscripted comedienne who created reels of Park memories? For example, in the summer of 1976, while the family was vacationing in Honolulu, for no apparent reason, she turned around and began running up the down escalator in the Ala Moana Mall. The mental footage entertained us for years, and she was a pretty good sport about it. I can still hear her trademark howl:

"I laugh butts-head off!"

Way too young, my dad's heart stopped in his sleep. To this day, I haven't recovered, but in 1979, my mom, not yet fifty with me half her age, I had work to do. In a way, took her husband's place. I handled the doctors, lawyers, taxes, and banking with her. We had fun outings, too: strawberry pie at the S&W Cafeteria and dim sum at The Ruby. Wherever we went, it was a table-for-two.

Neither her oldest nor favorite, I think a shrink might have a field day with me, but like most tragic stories, hers went deeper than text-book training, so deep it's a miracle that her kids, on some level, to some degree, like pups with second senses, got it: Our mom's cool heart was linked to her losing her long-ago first family, casualties of two wars. Her philosophy now: Life was *h-h-h-horrible*. Well, a daughter of missionaries ice-skating across the Yalu River in northern Korea in the midst of a magical childhood never expects to journey across the border alone at night with a stitch of bullets behind her, only to end up in 1950s America, land of Howard Johnson's famous hot dog but no kimchi. Now her soul floated between worlds—old Korea and modern American—with her heart more there than here, it seemed, in a stricken state that invaded her DNA and stole her maternal instinct to lovingly comb her daughters' hair the way I knew other mothers did. But anyone who paced the front porch with a car wreck of a face if you were even five minutes late but hugged your friend Lulu to near suffocation just because she got you home from college in one piece (was I seeing things?) loved her children more than God, and, trust me, she loved God a lot. Every night of motherhood, she fell into a prayer deep as a trance. If you accidentally walked in on her, she wouldn't wake up. *Uli* (our) Grace, *uli* Frances, *uli* Sammy, *uli* Ginger…

That said, if you came down with a cough, all hell broke loose. Later, we'd learn she was reliving memories of seeking a doctor, any doctor, in the tents, for her firstborn's relentless cough during the Korean War. *"She got whooping cough! Cough for hundred day! Almost die, I say! She j-j-j-just baby!"* But her overblown nursing skills on Layton Drive drove me to bury my cough in my pillow, and to this day, the smell of Campbell's Chicken Soup or Lipton Tea or Vicks makes me gag.

"All night I pray you not sick anymore. Stop c-c-c-cough!"

In the forty years following the death of my father, we carved out a little life for ourselves. By nature, I wasn't quite her cup of tea—too emotional for her tastes. Translation: weak. I knew better; that I was more like my dad, and in that way, my mom and I spoke different languages. But let me tell you, there were those moments when the whole neighborhood was asleep, and we talked into the late hour about the old days, hers there and ours here, when we were one candle, one flame. Entered a soulful universe. Because even though the world would change, and Koreans galore dotted the area so that whenever we drove back for a nostalgic peek at Layton Drive—we moved out in 1966 but stayed in the area—with the same two-trunked tree but not the neighbors, we would always feel like outsiders, if for no other reason than once-upon-a-time, the Parks were the only family that ate kimchi. My mom and I laughed loud, teased loud and yelled loud, nothing dainty here, and playfully called each other dumb-nuttys on a daily basis. Yes, I had boyfriends, too many, even a husband at one point, and how she despaired over my love life— *"You dumb-nutty, always like wrong man!"*— but she was my true partner. If I wasn't with her, I was missing her. Of course, my siblings, especially Ginger, shared their own golden spaces with her, rich as mine, but only they can tell their stories. Our space, I can tell you, was so sacred, words were a joke. We might be filling our baskets at Napoleon, her favorite Korean bakery, or clocking in at two hours on the phone until I'd hear her say, *"Hand hurt, talk too long."*

Over the course of four decades, as if she slowly crossed an ocean, my mom warmed up. Whispering sweet nothings would never be her thing, and if you gave her a hug, she didn't *quite* hug back. But she blew kisses from afar and penned lovey-dovey words in birthday cards. *"You are my wounderful* [sic] *daugher* [sic].*"* My guess is that she found peace with her fate, and though her heart still yearned for old Korea, she could finally feel the sun.

Last April, while playing a long and winding Korean card game on her sofa in the sitting room, my mom said she moved a funny way which caused a crippling pain in her back. *"J-j-j-just I twist!"* Doctors—an urgent care, her primary care, and a spine specialist who put her through five unnecessary procedures—failed to diagnose the cause of her pain for three months during which time, in ungodly agony, her beloved outings were limited to: a lunch at Han Gang Restaurant, a trip to Safeway, a final lunch at The Thai Café, and one final visit to Layton Drive, where we took pictures of the two-trunked tree a month before she could no longer move and an ambulance sped her to Fairfax Hospital, where, after her correct diagnosis, she underwent weeklong emergency radiation treatments before landing in hospice-at-home in July.

By the way, if you know nothing of metastasized lung cancer or end-of-life or active dying, run. Run like hell. Stay blissfully ignorant for as long as you can. Otherwise, you'll wish you were never born in the first place. Or, as my mom used to say: *"No one ask to be born but here we are, try to sorbibe."*

Ginger and I served as her round-the-clock hospice nurses. Despite the unimaginable moment in our lives, we dove into our roles. This was our mom, lost in a fog of post-hospital delirium, morphine, and every-nook-and-cranny cancer. One hour, she thought her legs were different countries; the next hour, she was wondering when Roger Federer was scheduled to play in the US Open. So, it was her and not her, stating frankly for the record: *"I like to lib fibe more year."* A far-fetched dream, but I still prayed for a miracle that she'd hang on for a few months and maybe—as her hopeful radiologist indicated—even walk again. Or at least be helped into a wheelchair and wheeled onto the deck just to breathe in her backyard, for God's sake. Take in the greenery. Was that too much to ask?

Apparently so.

One August day, at her bedside in a room far removed from Layton Drive, accepting the truth that our time was clocked, and my mom was poised to leave this universe for another, I buried my face in her neck and cried. Even then, I was self-conscious because tears never sat well with her. But she did the unexpected. As if pushing through fog, her right arm moved and began to pat my back slow and steady as she uttered in her most perfect English:

"My heart will always be with you."

Translation: I love you.

The next week, her arm was lifeless, as was she.

In the days and weeks that followed, I did what most of us do when we lose someone: I fell into my own fog. Slept too much and ate too little; had nightmares and waking dreams; smiled like a zombie would if it could; conjured up her hologram next to me. *"Dumb-nutty, you all alone now, go find b-b-b-better husband."*

The idea to make Christmas gifts for each of my siblings lifted the fog a little. Sometimes even just the thought could get me through the day, walk me from here to there. My plan: to frame vintage photographs of each sibling with our mom as a young mother.

After searching online, I ordered white marble frames—5x5 inch squares with cut-out heart spaces for the pictures—from World Market. When they arrived, I was happy with the museum quality but not the heart spaces; they were carved too deep, a good half-inch, at least. Considering the marble frame was so small to begin with, a photo might get lost in there. Look faraway. But I'd already spent hours combing the Park family archives for the perfect photos of yore, and my friend Jason had helped me scan and print them to size, so with tape and scissors, I went to work.

Done, each gift stood like a little memorial to our mom. The cut-out heart only added enchantment.

Mom.

There she is, cradling Ginger as a bonneted baby on Layton Drive next to the two-trunked tree. There she is, picking up Sam as a toddler at Bellevue Apartments. And there she is, a lifetime ago in her native country, holding hands with her firstborn Grace, small as a doll dressed in her tiny Korean *hanbok*. In a way, the last portrait stood out with its dreamy, ancient cast. But they were all special, and one night in mid-December, before wrapping them up, I took pictures of each one with my cell phone camera. That's when I noticed something on the screen. Something…odd.

In the old Korea image, the heart appeared raised, not engraved. Plump, like a real heart. Shocked stupid, I snapped more pictures from different angles, different lighting, even upside down. I scrolled through the images I'd just taken: same visual. I grabbed my laptop, focused the camera, click-click-click! More scrolling, more plump hearts. I was going nuts here. Possibly hallucinating.

After a long hard stare, more mystery: the hearts reverted to their true cut-out state, then began to slowly pulse up and down like . . . I'll just say it, a human heart. Double and triple-checked my vision, contacts in, contacts out, glasses on, glasses off. Every lens yielded the same result. Eventually, I printed off an image, doubtful the effect would transfer to paper.

It did.

Days passed before I mentioned a word of this to a soul. In fragile times, you don't need your sanity questioned. Eventually, I showed it to Jason.

"Do you see what I see?" I asked him.

He did.

The truth is, some might just see an optical illusion. Or nothing. But I see a gift from my mom, from her universe to mine. For forty years, we shared moments as one candle, one flame, one aura, and not even death is going to stand in our way. *"My heart will always be with you,"* she said—and I'm holding her to that.

AUTHOR BIO

Frances Park is the author or co-author of eleven books including the novels *When My Sister Was Cleopatra Moon* (Hyperion) and *To Swim Across the World* (Hyperion), the memoir *Chocolate Chocolate: The True Story of Two Sisters, Tons of Treats and the Little Shop that Could* (Thomas Dunne), the children's books *My Freedom Trip: A Child's Escape from North Korea* (Boyds Mills Press) and *Good-bye, 382 Shin Dang Dong* (National Geographic Books). Her short fiction and personal essays have been published in *O: The Oprah Magazine, Spirituality & Health Magazine, Chicago Quarterly Review, The London Magazine, Folio, The Massachusetts Review, Arts & Letters, The Belleview Literary Review, Gargoyle,* and *Coolest American Stories 2022*, to name a few. Interviews include National Public Radio, CNN, Good Morning America, Voice of America, and Radio Free Asia.

A finalist in the 2020 Dzanc Diverse Voices Book Prize and the 2019 Dzanc Novella Prize, Frances earned a spot on The Best American Essays 2017 Notable List with her essay, "You Two Are So Beautiful Together." Prizes for children's books include the International Reading Award, the Joan G. Sugarman Award, Notable Books for a Global Society Awards, and the Paterson Prize.

She also co-owns Chocolate Chocolate in downtown Washington, DC. Walk in and feel the magic.

And visit her at www.parksisters.com

CPSIA information can be obtained
at www.ICGtesting.com
Printed in the USA
LVHW041934170322
713623LV00005B/60